With my warmest regards
and love.

Kitty F. de Ruyter

"As I Have Loved You"

"As I Have Loved You"

by Kitty de Ruyter

Covenant Communications, Inc.

Published by Covenant Communications, Inc.
American Fork, Utah

Printed in the United States of America
First Printing: October 1994

01 00 99 98   10 9 8 7 6 5 4
Library of Congress Cataloging-in-Publication Data
de Ruyter, Kitty, 1937-
"As I have loved you" / Kitty de Ruyter.
p. cm.
ISBN 1-55503-707-0
1. De Ruyter, Kitty, 1937-   . 2. Mormon converts--Indonesia-
-Biography. 3. Persecution--Indonesia--History--20th century.
4. World War, 1939-1945--Indonesia--Prisons and prisoners, Japanese
I. Title.
BX8695.D47A3 1994
289.3' 092--dc20   94-33538
 [B]   CIP

Dedication

This book is written in honor of my mother, Anna Elisa, and to all mothers in similar situations who, like her, did their very best under difficult circumstances to be good, loving, and caring mothers, and succeeded because of their constant faith in the goodness and mercy of Heavenly Father.

This book is dedicated to my husband, Bob—my friend, my sweetheart, my "savior"; to my children—Erica, Scott, Rick, and Monica—and to their spouses; to my grandchildren, who were appointed to come to earth to live with our family, as gifts from Heavenly Father; and to Baboe Kit, and to all other baboes like her, who so lovingly, unselfishly, and devotedly cared for the children of others. She was truly my ever-remembered friend. *Sahabat-ku yang selalu di ingati.*

Dedication

This book is written in honor of my mother, Anna Elisa, and to all mothers in similar situations who, like her, did their very best under difficult circumstances to be good, loving, and caring mothers, and succeeded because of their constant faith in the goodness and mercy of Heavenly Father.

This book is dedicated to my husband, Bob—my friend, my sweetheart, my "savior"; to my children—Erica, Scott, Rick, and Monica—and to their spouses; to my grandchildren, who were appointed to come to earth to live with our family, as gifts from Heavenly Father; and to Baboe Kit, and to all other baboes like her, who so lovingly, unselfishly, and devotedly cared for the children of others. She was truly my ever-remembered friend. *Sahabat-ku yang selalu di ingati.*

PREFACE

Because our memories of events from the past may be dimmed over the years, it is always possible that these events will not be accurately retold. One's perspective changes as one grows older, and events are viewed from a difference angle, one that is enhanced by wisdom acquired through life's experiences.

It is not my intention to deceive or hurt people. While the events of which I write are based on my actual experiences, they are also gleaned from those of others; they are historically correct. The truth is that these things did occur. The names of certain persons have been changed to protect the innocent.

It is not my intention to dwell on the unfairness of war or to give a detailed scenario of the cruelty inflicted in this war, or to add to the suffering of those who are still struggling to rid themselves of the psychological or physical damage done to them because of the war, friend and foe alike. But rather my goal is to focus on the spiritual survival during such a difficult time and thereafter. It is to demonstrate the goodness and mercy of our Heavenly Father to many of His children who proved themselves valiant in their faith.

I have struggled with the decision to publish this book, because I myself have not lived a perfect life. I have made wrong choices, for which I have repented, and yet I have felt that my Heavenly Father has loved me through it all. I have truly felt His love encircle me. I have come to the conclusion that it is far better for the well-being of my peace to fight temptations rather than succumb to them and then have to bear the consequences, which are often painful to live with.

Nevertheless, how grateful I am for the knowledge that Heavenly Father loves me and that He knows me and cares about me. He has guided my life, prompted others to cross my path, so that we could each reach our destiny. He has enriched my life with trials and tribulations, blessed me with experiences beyond my expectations. He truly has performed miracles in my behalf. I deeply love Him and His Son, our Savior and Redeemer.

It is my profound hope that after reading this book, the reader will evaluate his or her own standing with Deity, then have the courage and determination to change and come unto Christ to love and serve Him. We will then understand the true meaning of His words:

"As I have loved you, love one another.
As I have served you, so serve one another."

ACKNOWLEDGEMENTS

My profound thanks and gratitude to my husband, Bob, for patiently and lovingly encouraging me to write this book, which has been a healing process in many ways, and for providing me with my own little corner with my very own word processor, which has forced me into the 90s.

My thanks also to my editor, Valerie Holladay, and the others at Covenant Communications who helped prepare this book, as well as to the many people I have met over the years who have asked me to write a book. Their letters of encouragement and their visits gave me the courage to write it.

Most of all, my deepest gratitude to my Heavenly Father for giving me the inspiration and the talents to write this story. It is my sincere wish to be an instrument in His hands to bring His work about.

How beautiful is youth,
How bright it gleams,
with its illusions,
aspirations, dreams. . . .

Henry Wadsworth Longfellow

A new commandment I give unto you,
That ye love one another;
as I have loved you. . . .

John 13:34

Chapter One

My life was very peaceful before war came to our little island in 1942 when I was eight years old. I was born in Semarang, on the island of Java, in Indonesia. The Indonesian islands curl along the equator like a string of pearls—south of the Philippines, north of Australia, and east and west of Singapore.

Each morning the sun peeked over the mountaintop and brought light to the dark morning, silhouetting the palm trees and other greenery, bringing color to them. The birds began to sing their sweet morning songs to awaken the world, and in the distance I could hear the crows from a proud rooster.

I envisioned paradise to be like this—peaceful, colorful, serene, and sweet-smelling. Everything was always so lush and colored in many nuances of green, enhanced by the perfume of many diverse varieties of flowers. No wonder Indonesia was called the "girdle of emeralds."

Every morning my nanny would call me, "*Selamat pagi, Nonny manis.* Good morning, sweet girl. Wake up, another day is here! *Ajoh, Nonny,*" Baboe Kit, my nanny, would come into the room and gently push open the mosquito curtains around my bed. But I just wanted to lie in bed a little longer, dreaming a young girl's dreams, and settled down cozily with my *gooling,* or bedroll, pulling up the flannel blanket against the cool tropical morning.

Baboe Kit was not young. Her teeth were reddish brown from chewing *sirih,* an extraction from the betel nut, a local custom. At night when her daily tasks were over, she would patiently pound the betel nut until it was smooth, and during the day she chewed it as one would use chewing tobacco. Baboe Kit wore a white *kebaya,* or overblouse, over her sarong, which smelled sweetly of the peculiar smell of the *sirih.*

How I loved this old face with the expressive big brown eyes. I often tried to picture her without the wrinkles around her eyes and mouth, and saw that she must have been a beautiful woman in her younger days. Her long hair was neatly knotted at the back of her head, with a big pin made out of teakwood stuck through the hair to keep it in place. She wore tiny silver pierced earrings and a nondescript pin on her *kebaya* to keep it closed. Yes, I loved my Baboe Kit dearly.

In the morning Baboe Kit would bathe me in our well-lit bathroom where stood a huge *mandi*—a trough made out of brick or cement—filled with water. The trough was large and deep enough to swim in; and when our nanny was not with us for a few moments, we children tried to do just that, much to her annoyance, for then they had to drain the water and clean the trough to have it ready for the next bathers. Baboe Kit would dry my body with a soft towel, then dust me with a sweet-smelling body powder and put my clothes on, which she had laid out on the dressing table beforehand. Then she would carefully brush and comb my hair, adorning it with a huge ribbon to match my dress or romper, all the while complimenting me on my beautiful hair and skin.

"You are a pretty girl," she would say, "but not too pretty to let it go to your head." She always spoke in soft, kind tones. I was a child with a destiny, she would tell me. If I would study well, be cheerful and kind, and take care of myself, I would marry well to a husband who would be as strong as seven water buffalo!

The reason that my nanny knew about these things was that she could read them in the palm of my right hand. She would carefully take my hand, stroke it a few times on the inside of the palm as if to study it carefully, then follow the middle line with her index finger and solemnly declare that I would have a long life and a magnificent future. She was so serious about this that I began to believe in these things, and I decided early in life that I would have to study hard and be good to deserve a good husband.

It helped me tremendously that my nanny kept telling me that I was a pretty girl, because I was the largest, the tallest, and the fattest of all my mother's girls, and I felt very self-conscious about that. My family used to call me "the chamber elephant" because they claimed they could hear and see me miles away.

To soften the harshness of this name, my family gave me the nickname "La Petite," which in French means "little one." My nanny, however, could not speak French and would call me *"Ittepetit" or Nonny manis,* which means "sweet little girl." Only when I was disobedient or when she could not find me would she call me by my given name, which is Kitty.

As all little children do, I loved hearing from Baboe Kit that she thought I was pretty; and because she pointed out so many pretty things in this world, I too learned to look at the pretty things. I learned to observe people and notice the color of their eyes and hair, the form of their noses and their mouths, the color of their skin (at least the different nuances of color), the shape of their hands—all their unique features. I became a people watcher and discovered at an early age that all people are God's creations. Because God is love, all good things come from him. He is our Creator, and what he creates is full of beauty, especially people. I had many questions about life and was very curious. Nanny seemed to have an answer for everything, or else she would refer me to my mother.

Baboe Kit was a very wise woman, and in my eyes she could do no wrong. Needless to say, I was very close to my nanny, who was a Muslim by faith as are many of the island inhabitants. Because my family was Christian, my mother counseled me to think of my Heavenly Father when my nanny would speak of Allah, and to think of the Lord Jesus Christ when she spoke of the prophet Mohammed. Nanny had the spirit of Allah, and I had the Holy Ghost. Both my mother and my nanny taught me to love God and to obey him.

Some days when I did not want to get up, I scooted towards the other side of the bed away from Baboe Kit.

"Adoe, nakal ja!" she would exclaim. "You are naughty—come to me now. It is time to get up, to wash, and to get dressed so you won't be late for prayers."

It was the custom in our home to start the day with a prayer, a scripture reading, a song, and a thought for the day before breakfast was served—and everyone was expected to attend and be on time! Our family belonged to the Dutch Reformed Church, a Protestant denomination, and all six children were taught from the Bible.

Each morning my father read to us from the Bible to teach us a concept or quality to emulate. His favorite book was John, perhaps because he had been named after this disciple by his foster parents, a missionary couple living in Magelang, Java. My mother's favorite scripture was from John 13:34-35: "A new commandment I give unto you, That ye love one another; as I have loved you, that ye also love one another. By this shall all men know that ye are my disciples, if ye have love one to another." And from 1 John 4:8, she taught us: "He that loveth not knoweth not God; for God is love."

After our daily scripture reading, we would sing a hymn, usually a familiar one that we children took turns choosing. My favorite song said, "Jesus says that he can see the light in our souls, whether it is bright and gives off lots of light, or only flickers as a candle about to burn out."

From my father I learned about Jesus, and I remember especially the story of Jesus meeting the woman at Jacob's well. Jesus offers the woman "living water" and says, "Whosoever drinketh of the water that I shall give him shall never thirst; but the water that I shall give him shall be in him a well of water springing up into everlasting life."

When Jesus tells the woman things that no one knows, she says, "I perceive that thou art a prophet," and he replies: "Ye worship ye know not what: we know what we worship; for salvation is of the Jews. But the hour cometh, and now is, when the true worshippers shall worship the Father in spirit and in truth: for the Father seeketh such to worship him. . . . And they that worship him must worship him in spirit and in truth." (John: 4:14, 19, 22-24.)

From this scripture I learned what a kind, loving man our Savior is. We cannot ever fool him; he knows everything we have ever done. And yet, he does not condemn us, but rather encourages us to drink from the living waters, that we may never thirst again.

After breakfast all the children attended school, even the little ones. Because we lived near our coffee plantation on the mountain, there were no public schools nearby. My parents hired tutors to teach the smaller children at home, but the older ones had to travel 45 miles to the city to attend middle and high schools. My parents preferred to send their children to private schools, so even though we were Protestants, the older children attended Roman Catholic schools run by the Catholic nuns, who were excellent teachers.

The Dutch, in order to keep the East Indies a colony, would not educate the native Indonesians, so very few had the opportunity to receive any form of education. Both my parents were well educated and education was very important to them, so they insisted that the children of their servants be educated alongside us. And so we ran a little school in our home, held in the west wing of the main house, which my mother had remodeled to accommodate all of these children. Our school was only half a day, usually until noon, because the temperature in the afternoon would climb so high that it was impossible to pay attention as we would become too sleepy.

We loved to have so many children come to the house and be our playmates! However, Mams cautioned us not to mimic their language, as these children did not speak Dutch very well and had come to school to improve their language skills. Our tutor had no problem keeping order in the little class, as everyone realized that going to school was a privilege and they wanted to make the most of it by studying hard and learning well.

During school, my Baboe Kit would often stay in my class, sitting on a three-legged stool close to the floor in the very back of the classroom. When she sat, Baboe Kit always made sure that her head was never higher than mine—a sign of submissiveness and respect for my status. She would absorb the teaching for an hour or so, listening intently, sometimes even giving the answers in her enthusiasm for learning, always remembering what was discussed or taught during the time she was in class.

My mother encouraged the nannies to attend class, but many were too self-conscious or too shy to come. That was not the case with my Baboe Kit, who was most eager to learn. When school was over, she would quiz me on the subjects we had learned that day. She was a real taskmaster, but it taught me to pay attention. Often we would write together, and I would become her teacher when I showed her how to make letters and numbers. My Baboe Kit was a very smart pupil.

After our recess break, the highlight of school for the children, Baboe Kit would attend to her other duties as a nanny—polishing my shoes, cleaning my rompers, tidying my bedroom, changing the sheets, and beating the mattress with a *sapoe lidi,* a broom made of long reeds.

Each of the children had a private baboe, or nanny. My nanny was Baboe Kit, because I was Kitty; the other nannies took the name of the child they cared for. Mams allowed them to choose between taking the name of a child or keeping their own, and they always chose a family name because of the prestige it gave them as well as a sense of belonging to the family they served.

My oldest brother was Konrad. He had dark curly hair, pensive dark eyes, and a gentle voice although he knew how to laugh! He was shy by nature but when he made friends he was fiercely loyal, and so he was well liked. At seventeen, he seemed very tall and strong to me.

Annalise, my oldest sister, was the fairest of all the children, with almost-blonde hair and a beautiful smile. She was smart as a whip and could talk a mile a minute. Mams gave her cooking lessons at an early age, although cooking was usually something only done by the servants. Mams and Annalise used the electric stove to make European and Indonesian food (the cook and her helpers preferred to cook our meals on wood or charcoal stoves). Annalise could bake the most delicious oatmeal and butter cookies! Her cakes were master-pieces!

My brother Herbert was very quiet and studious. He loved to read books and was always willing to read stories to the younger children. He was very inquisitive, almost as if he were driven by a need to know everything about the world—now! He loved to be near Mams; when he played with his tin soldiers, he always carried them into Mams' sewing room so that he could be near her as she sewed. Everywhere she went, he would follow her, talking to her and sharing his ideas with her. When the other children grew noisy, Mams would send us away to play outside or in another part of the house; but she never grew tired of having Herbie around her.

Daniel was my best pal. He was five years older than I with sparkling eyes and a contagious smile. He could never sit still for long and he always wanted to go off somewhere to explore. When we teamed up, I usually found myself in trouble—but it was worth it! We used to chase frogs and catch them, especially the large, fat ones (which could be as long as ten inches!), then throw them into the sparkling clean pool to frighten the swimmers!

One day Daniel and I hid from the baboes and walked to the

kali, or river, near the native village. "It's not hard to swim in the pool," Daniel said. "It's much more challenging to swim in the river." The *kali* was wide with a strong current. I wondered what we would do if we came upon a crocodile or some other ferocious animal. We were so far from the house; what would we do?

Daniel assured me that there were none and we climbed from rock to rock down into the river. Daniel swam like a fish and I wanted to follow him, until I remembered that I could not swim! So I dog-paddled after him, then climbed onto a rock. We tried to catch some pretty blue water flies and butterflies. Daniel showed me how to flip flat stones on the water. What fun we had! Then Daniel taught me to sing a naughty song, which went like this: "In the Orinoco was a crocodile, Who had a big boil on his left bum." "Bum" was a very naughty word to say, so we sang the word over and over again letting it echo back to us from the huge rocks on the other side of the river bank.

Our adventure ended abruptly when we heard voices coming from the bamboo groves behind us. We had been gone for hours, and my mother and the baboes had been worried about us, so Opa had taken several male servants to look for us. We heard Opa's thundering, raging voice, and we knew he was furious! We had left the house without permission and were playing in a dangerous river. Furthermore, tigers often hid in the bamboo groves near the river.

As punishment for our disobedience, Daniel and I could not leave our bedrooms; even our food was brought to us, in silence. Of course, I lost my appetite; I was too unhappy to eat. I could hear music and laughter coming from the sitting room area and knew that everyone else was having a good time and they were together. I was isolated. I learned that when rules are purposely broken, we have to pay the price. The price I paid was to be cut off from the family I loved. It was a horrible feeling. I wanted to be with my family again; I wanted them to trust me again. When we were able to return to the breakfast table two days later, we were not scolded again or teased by our siblings. We had repented and could now regain our place in the family unit.

Besides his adventurous, fun-loving side, Daniel had a sweet, spiritual nature. When Mams was expecting me, Daniel was very concerned about her. He was fascinated when Mams put his hand on her stomach and he could feel life in her belly as I kicked. Later, when Mams went to buy baby clothing for me, Daniel would pull her away from the blue baby outfits and insist that she buy pink outfits. "This baby is my little sister," he said. So Mams bought pink baby outfits and when I was born I was indeed Daniel's little sister!

My little sister Ellen was my mother's special girl. She had big brown eyes and a sensitive mouth. She was loyal and soft spoken, and was especially sensitive when she was teased for her dark skin. One day another child made fun of Ellen, and we all laughed—until I looked at Ellen's eyes and saw the hurt and pain in them. At home we never made fun of each other; my mother would not stand for that. So this was especially painful for Ellen, who was not used to such cruelty.

"Stop that," I said to Astrid, who was teasing Ellen. But she and the other children continued, even going so far as to make fun of Ellen's little nose. They had seen her reaction to their teasing and it was "fun." I pushed Astrid against her sister Sylvia, she pushed back, and before I knew it, I was punching everyone!

Ellen took this opportunity to escape. She reported the fighting to my mother, who sent Annalise out to investigate. My hair was tangled, the left sleeve of my dress was torn, and I had skinned my knee. Such were my feelings of love and loyalty to little Ellen. All my life I would be able to confide in her and share my innermost feelings.

My youngest brother Wim would not be born for some years yet.

This was my family. Our household also included many servants, cooks, and gardeners, as well as a chauffeur, who drove the older children to school every day. Our houseboy, Resoh, was our Number One servant and had been with my mother's family for many, many years. He was nearly 70 years old and could even remember when my mother had been a little girl. He knew just how to push my chair in to the table at mealtimes so that I could have good posture! He would pull my chair from the table and put a pillow on the seat, then push me close to the table. I would smile my thanks to him, and he would nod his head in acknowledgment, then stand back against the wall in his white jacket and colorful sarong, his eyes constantly alert to see where he could be of service. Sometimes when I left the breakfast table to say goodbye to my older siblings as they went off to school, Resoh would clear away my morning oatmeal. I was always overjoyed when I found he had done so, as I didn't particularly care for breakfast.

Fresh fruits grown in our own orchard were always available—usually pineapple, papayas, mangistan, bananas, grapefruits, oranges, and even occasional strawberries. Eggs for breakfast were usually soft-boiled, served in pretty china egg cups with pearly egg spoons because silver spoons would tarnish when used to eat eggs. When we had guests, there was always special food served—home-baked breads and sausage rolls, thin Dutch pancakes served with powdered sugar, jams, all kinds of cheese, and meats or sausages. My favorite dish was rice porridge cooked in coconut milk and garnished with brown cane sugar, which I could eat seven days a week!

When we had visitors, Mams would have lunch served in the big dining room or on the veranda, which encircled half of our house. There our guests could enjoy our beautiful view of the terraced ricefields below and our own terraced rose gardens. In the distance was a beautiful, almost aquamarine-colored lake, the Rawah Pening. The pillars of our veranda were covered with white stephanotis, a sweet-smelling flower, and an abundance of red and pink bougainvillea.

The guests would sit in the oversized white rattan chairs with their colorful pillows, enjoying the view and visiting with my father, who was obviously content that he was able to provide so well for his family. A businessman who often entertained guests, my father preferred to bring them to our home rather than put them up in the city. They would usually stay in one of our guest houses near the swimming pool or tennis courts, but would come to the main house for their meals.

We children learned a lot by listening to their conversations, especially when business matters were discussed. It was fascinating to hear about where our visitors lived or where they had traveled, and we listened quietly to their stories. When our guests were foreigners from Europe, our knowledge of foreign languages was tested. It was mandatory for us to speak in the language of our guests! Even the little ones had to be able to at least greet guests in their native tongue.

At times when we did not have visitors, the children would eat in the big kitchen with the baboes and the kitchen helpers. I loved to sit with them and listen to the latest gossip about the other Indo or Dutch families in our hamlet. The baboes would go to the *passar,* which is the open marketplace, and come back with news of the village. In this way we learned of local happenings, such as when *kebun* Hodjono, one of our gardeners, became engaged to Suki, the pretty baboe who worked for the Gilderas family, who lived just below us on the mountain. This meant that there would be a *selamatan,* or celebration soon in the *kampong,* and we would be invited to come! We could look forward to being entertained by a *gamelang* orchestra with its mysterious sounds, a *wajang* puppet show, and many wonderful things to eat!

We also celebrated both Christian and Muslim holidays. At Christmas we had a beautiful tree, decorated with beautiful colored glass ornaments and dazzling white candles in their candle holders and glass silver birds, with long tails. The most mysterious part of the Christmas tree was the white cotton at the foot of the tree, which was supposed to be snow. We had no snow in our tropical paradise, and I only knew that snow was a "woolly sort of ice" that felt very cold when you picked it up. I knew that it snowed in faraway Holland, our motherland, and that it was very cold because rivers and canals would be covered with ice.

At the Islamic New Year we would be invited by the people in the *kampong* to come celebrate. On the east side of our compound was an Islamic cemetery, and on the day of feasting, people would gather at the cemetery to remember their kindred dead and offer the most wonderful food imaginable. They also had a celebration for the living, because we would always be invited to come feast with the baboes.

Brought up with the influence of both Muslim and Protestant, I had the best of both worlds. I was never confused by them, as I knew which one was which. I was a Protestant, and I firmly believed that I was a daughter of God and a follower of Christ.

Chapter Two

Like Nephi of old, I too came from goodly parents. In my youth I was taught to love God and have faith in him, and I saw how the scriptures came to life because of examples of righteous living.

Mams was soft-spoken and always hummed a song or hymn as she worked. I never heard her utter a profane word of any kind. She had fair skin inherited from her Dutch father, and soft, fawnlike brown eyes. She preferred to wear her naturally wavy, dark brown hair cut short and parted in the middle.

I can best describe my mother by quoting the Apostle Paul:

. . . He that giveth, let him do it with simplicity; he that ruleth, with diligence, he that showeth mercy, with cheerfulness.

Let love be without dissimulation. Abhor that which is evil; cleave to that which is good.

Be kindly affectioned one to another with brotherly love; in honor preferring one another.

Not slothful in business; fervent in spirit; serving the Lord;

Rejoicing in hope; patient in tribulation; continuing instant in prayer;

Distributing to the necessity of saints; given to hospitality.

Bless them which persecute you; bless, and curse not.

Rejoice with them that do rejoice, and weep with them that weep." (Rom. 12:8-15)

My mother loved beauty and surrounded us with it. We began each day in beauty, gathering in our dining room for prayers and breakfast. My mother loved plants and flowers, so the dining room held palms in huge Chinese urns, ming trees, and other ornamental plants. An abundance of flowers decorated the sideboard and each of the round tables in the sitting area in front of the bay windows. The massive Chinese ebony table in the middle of the room was covered with a cheerful pale yellow/gold damask tablecloth, and in the middle of the table was a floral arrangement consisting of anthuriums, birds of paradise, gerberas, white lilies, and greens in a Chinese bowl. The china always glistened, the crystal sparkled, and the silverware shone. The napkins were artfully folded like fans on the plates.

The big chairs around the table, in their peculiar Chinese shape, were upholstered in gold brocade with blue-green peacocks. Along the wall opposite the windows was a long shelf filled with books, Chinese ming vases, decorative plates, and two huge black onyx elephants with real ivory tusks. On the tiled floor lay a huge woolen rug in a Chinese pattern in blue and green motifs with a pale pastel background. Above the room hung an elegant, sparkling chandelier.

Mams worked closely with the servants to supervise their duties. She would write up lists of groceries, meat, and vegetables for the kitchen helper to buy at the local open marketplace and would give her money to spend. Mams always treated the servants with respect and trust; therefore, few would cheat her out of the extra money.

The people in the village lovingly called my mother *Bonda Bomo* or *Ibu Doktor,* which means "Mother the doctor." Mams healed a village baby from malaria when the holy man from the village had given up. Another time, a tree fell on Si Sudarman, our gardener, during a severe thunderstorm and his legs were crushed. Mother was summoned to the village, where she set his legs as best she could. Infection set in and he healed very slowly. His hallucinations and delirious cries could be heard outside of his hut, and the villagers thought that he was beset by evil spirits.

My mother nursed him back to health and taught his mother to massage his legs so that he could walk again using crutches. He still needed a cane to get around, but he was able to work—not doing gardening work, but doing odd jobs around the house such as polishing the silver, watering the plants, and cleaning pots and pans in the kitchen where my mother could keep an eye on him to make sure that he would not abuse his legs by overdoing it.

There were many of these stories, and the people truly believed that my mother had healing hands.

We also learned that our mother was very courageous, as her longtime childhood friend Lien told us how as a school girl, Mams had seen a group of boys taunting two boys who were fighting. When she discovered that one of the boys was her brother Herbert, who was being badly beaten up, she rushed over to the group and learned that one of the boys had made fun of Herbert, making a crude remark about their mother and father, and Herbert had stood up in defense of them. Herbert was not a strong boy, as he still suffered from the effects of his life in the *dessa*.

My mother had challenged the bully to fight her rather than her brother, and he had refused. However, she had insisted and thrown the first punch. After a long fight, my mother had won! She warned the boys never to utter a word against her mother or father, and to leave her brother alone.

That was the courage my mother had!

And how we loved it when, during the dinner hour, our father would describe his work and what he did all day away from home at his business. Our favorite stories were those of his youth.

Oh, the things my father used to do as a boy! He told us how when he was away at school, his classmates and he used to sneak through an opening in the hedge around the schoolyard to buy snacks at nearby foodstands. My father's favorite snack was *roedjak*, an assortment of young fruit with a very hot dressing over it, usually a mixture of sweet soy sauce, spices, and hot peppers. Because they were on borrowed time, they could not savor their food and had to eat it quickly.

Back in the classroom, their mouths still burned from the hot, peppery dressing and they had to put their hands or handkerchiefs over their mouths and blow to cool their mouths. Drinking water would have been disastrous, as it would merely have moved the hot pepper down the throat and burned the esophagus. Sometimes the teacher would ask one of the boys to read before the class, which meant that he had to stop blowing—and how could he read while his mouth was burning up? The teacher would, of course, ask, "What is the matter with you?" and the student would have to confess, then bear the consequences of his deed, especially the humiliation of being caught.

When our father told these stories, we would giggle until our bellies ached. We discovered that our father was a fun dad, but he also used these stories to teach us valuable lessons—that it does not pay to be disobedient, as sooner or later one will get caught and have to pay the price.

I thought my father was the most handsome daddy in the whole world, and I loved and admired him. He never spoke harshly or raised his voice in anger.

Our father was a foundling, found on a railroad track by Pa VanderSteur. Pa and Ma VanderSteur were a missionary couple who took Euro-Asian children into their orphanage. Pa VanderSteur would often travel to nearby *dessas*, or native villages, to preach Christianity. When he saw fair-skinned children amidst the brown-skinned natives, he would inquire about them as it was common for many Euro-Asian children to live in the *dessas* nameless and neglected because they were not acknowledged by their European fathers, and often their mothers were not able to care for them.

If Pa VanderSteur could locate the mother of one of these Euro-Asian children, with her permission he would take the child home, give him a name, and raise him as a European child. The VanderSteurs educated their foster children, but more importantly, they gave them stability as well as an identity. The "Steurtjes," as the children called themselves, were extremely loyal to their "parents" and to each other. When war came to Indonesia, the Steurtjes kept in contact with each other and helped each other. In Holland after the war, my mother assisted other Steurtjes, showing the loyalty and generosity that my father would have shown had he been alive.

My father often visited the VanderSteurs' home, bringing gifts and treats for the children. Sometimes he would bring us children along, and those visits taught us to be grateful to have our own father and mother who were able to raise us themselves. We were glad that our father was so protective of us. Because he had had to go without so many things, he wanted us to have the best things, but at the same time, not to take them for granted.

My grandfather, whom we called Opa, also lived with us. He was a tall man, his back straight as a ramrod, with a light complexion tanned by the sun, white hair, and a neatly-trimmed white moustache. He always wore his metal-rimmed eyeglasses through which his sparkling deep blue eyes peered. His voice was deep but always gentle and kind, and he had wonderful large hands with long, slender fingers.

The villagers spoke reverently about my grandfather, and called him the *Tuan besar*, which means the respected or honorable gentleman. One day he chased a tax collector out of the village who had become greedy and demanded more goods from the people to pay for their so-called "taxes." The tax collector had some official-looking papers, which he said allowed him to confiscate goods from the people, but Opa could read and saw that they had nothing to do with the seizure of property.

Opa reminded me so much of Heavenly Father. I somehow always pictured my Heavenly Father to look like my grandfather—tall, slim, with white hair and a deep, quiet voice. He was kind, gentle, and ever-forgiving, full of love and compassion, wise and all-knowing.

One day, when I was supposed to be napping as the day was so very hot, I took the opportunity to wander about my parents' vast estate. My parents had set strict boundaries where we could and could not go, and had warned all the children to abide by their rules. Nevertheless, I was happy taking my doll, Pop Mientje, for a walk and found myself in "forbidden" territory near our pool and guest bungalows. When the path ended at the gate to the swimming pool, I decided to walk along the top of the embankment surrounding the pool area. As I made my way carefully, my foot slipped off the wall, and my doll and the stroller and I all tumbled down the steep embankment, landing in the vegetable garden on the second terrace.

Oh, how I hurt! I had cut my forehead and scratched my legs, and began to cry out for help. I dared not called out for my mother or nanny, because I knew I would be punished for being so disobedient as to come into this area unescorted. Besides, I knew that I was too far from the main house for them to hear me, so I lay there and wailed pitifully.

Suddenly it came to me that even if everybody would be angry with me for my willful disobedience, my Heavenly Father would still love me. So I said a prayer to ask him to come help me. When I opened my eyes, I saw the blood dripping from my forehead onto my lap and instinctively began to cry even louder, "Somebody please help me!"

I looked up and saw a tall man with white hair, dressed in tropical whites, walking towards me with long, dignified strides. It was my grandfather, Opa, who came to my rescue and gently scooped me up in his wonderful arms. Not a cross or accusing word was uttered, only soothing and comforting words, accompanied by kisses.

He carried me to his big garden shed, where he loved to experiment and develop hybrid flowers and plants. He had graduated from the higher horticultural school in Wageningen, Holland, and was working on a project with the vanilla plant, and its beans and flowers smelled so delicious in his shed.

He sat me on a chair and wiped the blood from my face with his handkerchief. He gave me a glass of cool water to drink and then bandaged my forehead with gauze and tape. He saw to my needs first, then knelt eye-to-eye with me. In ever so gentle tones, he told me that he loved me dearly and that my parents were loving parents. "You know that your Pappie and Mammie love you and your brothers and sisters," he said. "That's why they have set up certain rules, which are for your safety and protection and to teach you obedience. They want you to be safe and happy. If you are disobedient, you could hurt yourself or have an accident, and we would be so unhappy."

Did I understand now why it was forbidden to walk alone in the pool area? he asked. I could have fallen into the pool and drowned. As it was, I had fallen off the embankment on the other side and was lucky not to have been hurt more severely. I nodded my head in shame and promised that I would not walk there alone anymore and would stay on the paths. Opa looked at me closely when I spoke these words, and I knew that he trusted me and expected me to keep my word. Because I loved my grandfather, I vowed I would keep my word.

In later years, when I was in difficulty or in mental anguish, and I would cry out to my Heavenly Father for help, the image of this scene with my grandfather would come to my mind. In those times, I would actually feel as if my Heavenly Father had picked me up, folded me into His arms, and pressed me against His bosom. I could lay my head on His shoulder and cry my heart out and tell Him my anguish, and somehow speaking to Him would quiet and comfort my heart and bring peace to my soul. I would feel safe and secure in His love, no longer alone, deserted and forsaken, as I could feel His love permeate my whole body. With this reassurance of my Heavenly Father's love, I knew what I needed to do to solve my problem. I had to take action. But first, it was necessary to love Him with all my heart, mind, and soul, above all things and above anybody—even myself. "If ye love me, keep my commandments," He had said, and so I had to start with keeping all of His commandments to the fullest of my ability.

What a blessing to have such a magnificent grandfather, one whose life I could liken to that of my Heavenly Father, a picture which has strengthened and fortified me in time of need throughout my life.

After he had sweetly comforted me and gently chastised me, Opa took me to find my rag doll and then walked me slowly toward the main house. My grandfather always took slow paces so that we children could keep up with him. He always gave us time to look around, and never rushed us.

We arrived at the house and learned that Baboe Kit had been searching frantically for me everywhere. When she saw us she ran to us, bowed to my grandfather, and begged his forgiveness for her negligence. Opa spoke kindly to her, reassuring her that she was not to blame. I could see that she had been crying, and I felt horrible that I had been so selfish not to think of her. "I'm so sorry, Baboe Kit," I said. "I will never do that again!" She did not scold me. She blamed herself, and that was worse. "I'm just so glad you are all right," she kept saying.

I watched my grandfather walk to the other side of the house to his own quarters. As if he felt my gaze on his back, he turned around and waved, smiling at me, and I waved back.

My grandfather was a generous and compassionate man. Everyone loved and respected him. He contributed large amounts of money toward the building of a hospital in the nearby town of Salatiga, and at his own expense, had sent two Indo students to Europe to study medicine so that they could come back to Indonesia and practice medicine. This was because there was a severe shortage of good medical doctors in the colonies; the Dutch doctors would stay only a short time because they could not handle the tropical climate.

My grandfather never married. In those days, marriages between a Dutch citizen and a native woman of the colonies was not recognized by the Dutch government. Karsih, the Javanese mother of Anna, my mother, and her brother, Herbert, decided to return to her village to live, and it was unthinkable for a Euro-Asian child to live with the mother in her native village. Because my grandfather had acknowledged his children, this meant that they could be registered and receive a birth certificate issued by the Dutch Indonesian colonial authorities. (Euro-Asian children were considered Dutch citizens only when acknowledged by the Dutch father.)

Since Opa traveled extensively, he did not feel that he could adequately raise his children himself while being gone so often. So when Anna and Herbert were a little older, he made arrangements for them to be boarded with the Wurthingtons, a trustworthy Christian family whom he felt would give them the best education available and ensure that his children would not lack any material things.

Opa visited Anna and Herbert frequently, coming into town unexpectedly to check on the Wurthingtons and to see if the children were treated fairly. During the school vacations, Opa would take them to the plantation or to the village of Batu in the mountains, and these were always happy times for my mother and her brother. My mother loved her father very much and missed him deeply when he was not around.

Mother admitted to me years later that she did not have a happy childhood with the Wurthingtons. They meant well, but she didn't feel that she was part of the family. Many times she did not get the clothes that were promised to her, and had to make do with hand-me-downs or makeovers. She never complained and pretended that she did not care about clothes, and because of her nonchalant attitude, she was considered a "tomboy." In reality, however, she wanted to be a lady, with pretty clothes and ribbons in her hair. Above all, she craved to be held and loved by a mother. She wanted to live with her own mother; but Karsih had left my grandfather to return to her village to marry someone else, and, as mentioned, Euro-Asian children did not live with their mothers in the native village.

As a child, my mother attended a private Roman Catholic school, although she herself was not Catholic. The school was considered one of the best available in mid-Java, educationally as well as socially, and the nuns were very strict. After she graduated, she went on to receive her pharmaceutical certificate from the university.

Her brother Herbert studied music in Europe after graduating from high school in Indonesia. He became an accomplished violinist, playing with the Brussels Philharmonic Orchestra and later traveling through Europe as a featured soloist. During vacations, he often visited us in Indonesia.

Opa also had two sons, James and John, from another beautiful native woman, Nadikum. James and John were much younger than my mother, and she took them into her home and raised them as her own. Although Nadikum moved back to her own village, she often visited Opa, and we were always thrilled to have her come visit as she was so beautiful and full of life. She always brought baskets of fruits and treats. She was the closest to a grandmother that we had.

My mother played the piano and insisted that all the children take piano lessons, so we developed a love for music at an early age. We were a happy family, and our evenings were always filled with music and song with Mams at piano, Uncle Herbert on the violin, Uncle James on the Hawaiian guitar, and my father on the mandolin. My Uncle John drummed on the table. We children all sang at the top of our lungs. We sang Indo folk songs, love songs, Hawaiian songs, and often hymns. When the grown-ups harmonized, we were happy to listen. Even the servants could not resist sitting in the corridor to listen and enjoy the fun.

When Uncle Herbert would play "hillbilly" music on his concert violin, Opa would joke that he had not spent a fortune to send his son to Europe to learn hillbilly music. But we knew that Opa enjoyed it, nonetheless.

Yes, we were a fun-loving, happy clan. I was so glad to be a part of this family.

Chapter Three

Baboe Kit believed in many evil spirits, of which Satan was the largest and the most evil. She called them *Setan Goedoel, Loentil Anak, Goendorowah*, as well as by other names. All the baboes could make me feel uneasy with their spooky stories about their evil spirits and their fortune tellings. Part of me knew that it was all nonsense; and yet, another part of me warned that some of it could come true. My own Baboe Kit had predicted that I would marry a *blanda*—that is, a Dutchman, as *blanda* means white. "*Adoe*, no more spicy hot food for you, Nonny!" the baboes would tease me and giggle as they knew that I was crazy about good, spicy, hot Indonesian food. Just in case they were right in their predictions, I decided to take precautions.

The baboes had warned me not to eat leftovers out of a black iron pan, because eating too much out of a black pan would cause me to marry a very dark man. I didn't care about that because I knew the color of his skin didn't matter as much as whether he was a good man. But now I had a reason to eat as much as I could from a black pan. I wanted to have a dark husband—one who would love hot, spicy Indonesian food. So I would go into the kitchen and scrape food from the bottom of the blackest pot to fulfill the prediction that I would marry a dark man so I would not have to give up my hot, spicy food. (It never occurred to me that I might marry a *blanda* who would love this food. My wonderful *blanda* husband loves Indonesian food and often teases me that he only married me because I could cook it so well!)

Both Indos and Indonesians are fascinated with fortune-telling, and our neighbor who lived on the foot of the mountain, Mrs. van Zonnen, claimed that she had the power to look into the future through cards and palmreading. One day when we paid a visit, she held a seance, and naturally love and romance was foretold for all the young adults, complete with descriptions of future suitors, all given with much laughter and joking. Only after much persuasion did my mother subject herself to this "nonsense," as she called it. Although she was reluctant to allow herself to be the center of attention, we children were most anxious to hear what her future would bring.

Mams picked seven cards and handed these to Mrs. van Zonnen, who smilingly accepted them at first; but then her face grew serious as she spread the cards on the table, moving them around from one end to the other. She shook her head a few times, and studied the cards some more. "This is not good, not good at all. Look at these cards! Your house of cards is going to cave in—in other words, you will lose your home and all your possessions!"

"How?" Mams asked, although she was not alarmed by this "prediction." "Through earthquakes, mudslides, fire? Can you be more specific?"

Perhaps Mrs. van Zonnen did not know, or perhaps she did not want to say, because she turned to a new prediction.

"Anna, I see also that you are going to travel far away from here—overseas," she said before she picked up the cards, absent-mindedly shifted them, and put them away in the box. "Give me your hand, Anna," she then demanded of my mother, who complied. "Ah, this better. You will live a long life, Anna. I see obstacles, but you will live a long life. *Adoe*, I see many tears, deep sorrow, men in uniform, there is fire! And you will go away from here on a long trip. These men in uniform surround you!" Then, in direct contrast to what she had been saying, Mrs. van Zonnen said, "The Lord bless you, Anna! You are well loved, Anna. Many, many love you! This is *betul, betul*. This is the truth, Anna."

"Thank you," Mams said graciously, and then said, "I believe that we finally will make that trip back to Belgium on furlough, to attend Herbie and Antoinette's wedding!" Mams explained. "That takes care of this long trip you are talking about."

"Oh, *adoe*, Anna, wait," Mrs. van Zonnen said. "There are tears and sorrow. How can this be? These people in uniform that surround you! I see a sword—a sword, Anna. Look at these lines in your hand!" She went on for a while, which made me quite nervous.

Finally Mams stood up and said, "I know that you truly believe in these things. But I also know what I believe. Let me give you my interpretation of your prediction." I knew Mams would make light of these foreboding words, if only to make us feel better. "When we go on furlough to Belgium and Holland, which is the trip overseas, we will be invited by the Queen for an audience at the palace. There will be an honor guard who will surround us, and then the Queen will knight me with a sword to be the Queen of Sheba. Then I shall have to give up this good life, as I will have to attend to my "queenly" duties, which will sorrow me and bore me to tears! There, now you have the true interpretation."

Turning to Mrs. van Zonnen, Mams said, "Zonnetje, thank you for your reading. I expect that I will live a long life. I have all these children to raise, and I do believe that I will find obstacles along the way which may bring me sorrow and tears. I also know that many love me, because I have many children and they love me. You are a good fortune teller."

We stayed for a while longer to visit, then taking us children by the hand, she led us home. I felt much better now. I was very glad that my mother had interpreted her own future. All these ominous predictions had made me nervous and uneasy.

Just to be sure, I asked my mother if fortune tellers really could see into the future. "Some do," she said, "but it is not meant for men to know their future. There would not be any surprises left in life if we knew our future. Sometimes we would be afraid to continue to live. If people knew that a bad day was ahead of them, they would roll over in their beds and not get up to face that bad day. People would not go to work that day, and there would be chaos on earth. They would not know and learn that when one turns a bad day into a good day, one develops a strong character and becomes a better person. One needs to go through a bad day to appreciate a good day.

"Remember, Kitty, that only good things come from God, and God wants us to have peace in our souls and be happy people. If we knew beforehand what lies ahead of us, we might become too frightened to live and worry ourselves to death because we could not change this 'future,' no matter what we would do."

Those were wise words, and I decided that I did not want to know my future. I just did not want to know, for example, on what day a tiger could come and eat me. I'd rather be surprised and get it over with, and not have to stew about it for years. That was a wise decision.

Chapter Four

Two things happened to change my life on the island. First, the Germans invaded Holland on May 10, 1940. Holland had declared herself "neutral" during this conflict, but the Germans needed Rotterdam, a large harbor, to get access to the North Sea. Holland's military forces were ill-equipped to withstand the German troops, who, ignoring their neutral status, overran the tiny country. The inner city of Rotterdam was completely leveled by the German bombs. To avoid the same destruction in other cities, Holland capitulated only five days after the invasion. The queen and her cabinet fled to Great Britain, leaving the Dutch without a government but maintaining radio contact with the underground.

Our family huddled around the shortwave radio, trying to catch any news from Holland. Mrs. MacGillefrey called all the neighbors together to pray for the Dutch in our motherland. Meanwhile, the Dutch East Indies prepared herself for war, and training in the military proceeded in full force. Because all able-bodied men over the age of eighteen were inducted, and because our economic ties with Holland were now severed, the economy virtually came to a standstill. My Uncle Herbert, who had come to visit us, could not return to Holland.

During this chaotic time, all communications with Holland were interrupted or intercepted, and there was no guidance or direction. However, with great courage and dedication, the Dutch-Indonesian government formed a coalition and took matters into their own hands, thus giving us a form of leadership.

My father and my uncles—except Uncle Herbert, who was rejected by the military—were drafted into the armed forces, and we did not see them for days, sometimes weeks. The women rallied together and helped each other as best they could. Many of our neighbors and friends relied heavily on my mother. Mrs. MacGillefrey, or Auntie Teresa as we called her, lived on the other side of the cemetery from us. My mother spent many hours in her house, helping her to take care of her affairs.

During this time, my mother dreamed a particularly strong dream over and over again and she could not keep this dream out of her mind. She dreamed that she was instructed to build a bomb shelter, and she felt so strongly about the dream that she hired a laborer from the village to build it. Now, the Dutch East Indies were not at war and there was really no threat of war in the air, although the military were prepared to defend their motherland if necessary. In the dream, she was instructed to build the shelter right next to the main house. And even though bomb shelters are usually built far away from the house in case the house is bombed, my mother insisted that the shelter be built directly adjacent to the house. In fact, it was so close to the house that it connected to a secret passage to our wine cellar. The spot that Mams chose was the place where my father had planted roses, imported all the way from England, to commemorate their wedding anniversary. So the roses had to be uprooted and planted somewhere else.

The bomb shelter was filled with food, mostly dehydrated, with a large variety of vegetables and fruits that had been dried in the hot sun on flat baskets. There were sacks and sacks of rice put away, barrels of water, medicine, extra clothing, shoes and blankets—all according to the instructions of the dream. She even stored her black medical bag in the shelter, just in case. The bag was filled with medicine, bandages, razor blades, medical instruments, scissors, a sewing kit, and a container of *haagse hopjes*, which was a favorite coffee candy of hers. Her black bag also held two hair clippers, as she was often asked to give haircuts to the village children when she was visiting the sick.

The second event that changed my world occurred on December 7, 1941. Japan attacked Pearl Harbor and declared war on the United States of America and her allies, in part because the U.S. had leveled an embargo against Japan in retaliation for their aggressive and destructive invasion of Korea and China.

Because of their involvement in the war, Japan needed oil, and turned toward the Dutch East Indies, who had plenty of oil. We expected the Japanese to invade Indonesia, as they had already defeated the Americans in the Philippines, and the Dutch East Indies government declared a state of emergency. When the Japanese arrived in waves of military strength, there was only a short period of formal resistance. Even with the help of some Australian troops who had come to our defense, we were no match for the Japanese troops who quickly overcame our military forces and placed all military personnel behind barbed wire and all Europeans in concentration camps to prevent any acts of sabotage. Everyone was detained except those who could prove German citizenship.

People were picked up off the streets at random, without being given the chance to notify their families or relatives. Teenage boys were separated from their families and put in separate boys' camps. Many died of starvation, dehydration, or disease. The Japanese emptied the prisons in order to fill them with captured civilians while the now freed prisoners stole openly and committed other crimes.

Times were hard for everyone. All bank accounts were frozen and no wages earned. We had no money to buy necessities. We could no longer pay our servants, and my mother stood at the gate to prevent our faithful employees from coming to work for us. Some ignored her and continued to come and work for nothing, especially those who cared for the cows. These servants would come and milk the cows early in the morning and in the afternoon, and they even taught Annalise and Konrad how to milk as well. Mams divided the milk with these faithful, kind natives.

Annalise loved the animals and cared for them diligently, even under the most dire circumstances. When the servants weren't able to come, Annalise was the one who went to the meadows, followed by her little Pekinese dog, Yoto, to milk the cows.

It was too dangerous to travel any distance from home, as we could be picked up from the street and thrown in a prison camp. But as we no longer had a kitchen helper to go to the open market for us, my mother devised a plan to "shop" for food. At least three times a week we would stand along the thoroughfare from the little village to the marketplace in town, and she would call out to the villagers that she wanted to buy their wares. In this manner we bartered for our necessities with our soy sauce, eggs, butter, milk, fruits, and especially salt, which proved a most desirable commodity to barter with. Salt had to come from the mines, and there was no transportation. But Mams had wisely stored a large quantity of salt along with the other food items in her storage shelter.

It was not always safe to stand there on the roadside, as the Japanese often drove by in their trucks and confiscated everything in sight. My mother made a game of it for us children. She would put each of us "in charge" of a particular barter item, which we would hide in the bushes. When a deal was struck, she would call us and we would bring the item to her to exchange it for her "purchase." Tante Lien, my mother's friend, lived on the thoroughfare and extended to us an open invitation to use her house as refuge when it became dangerous to stay in the street.

All of the children learned to contribute to our family welfare. Annalise made oatmeal cookies and cakes to be sold to our neighbors; Konrad sold milk, butter, and cheese. One day, one of our cows gave birth to a calf, and her milk was orange instead of white. Mams made special butter out of that orange milk and divided it among the neighbors. It had a very special meaning to all of us, because our Dutch queen belonged to the House of Orange. So we celebrated her birthday, which we called "Queensday," a little early with our orange butter! Our secret celebration, held right under the noses of our invaders, gave us all a boost.

The happy feeling did not last long, however. Opa was getting older and forgetful. At first he spent most of the time in his room, reading or sleeping. But as time went on, Opa would not even get out of his bathrobe all day, and my mother had to coax him to eat or take any nourishment. He became disoriented and lost weight rapidly.

One day, a military car and truck unexpectedly came up the mountain road and approached our compound. We knew that the Japanese would even take away the older men to work in the camps, and my mother was naturally concerned about the safety of her father. Quickly she instructed my brother and our houseboy, who had steadfastly refused to leave us, to move the grand piano from the music room against the bedroom door. "That way it doesn't look like a bedroom," she told them as she placed a large vase with flowers on the piano to conceal Opa's bedroom door. Then she smoothed out the carpet so as not to leave any trails from the piano wheels.

A few moments later, a Japanese officer and four soldiers stepped on the veranda to enter our home. The Japanese soldiers often broke down front doors as a show of intimidation and power, but my mother was quicker than they were. She opened the big door for them and invited them to come in. The soldiers carried rifles with uncovered bayonets and placed themselves near each door of the room and the front door, ready to block each entrance.

The officer had a short leather whip that he slapped into his gloved hand while moving about the room, picking up art pieces, looking at them as if he were shopping in a store, moving paintings on the walls aside as if to see if they concealed a secret storage place. All the while, he rapidly asked questions of my mother, sometimes asking her the same questions twice or three times, trying to trip her in her answers. Mams remained calm and composed, her appearance smooth and unruffled. He watched her carefully, observing her reactions.

"Where is your husband?" he asked repeatedly. "What does he do for a living? Where was he educated? What is his work, that he can afford such fine art pieces?"

"I don't have a clue where my husband is. I haven't heard from him," she replied. She turned the question back to him. "Do *you* know where he is, and if he is safe?" Then, as an afterthought, she boldly asked, "If you find out where he is, will you come and tell me? I do worry a great deal about him."

The officer did not reply but continued walking about the room. Stopping abruptly at the wall bookcase, he took out a book, turned some of the pages and read them. The book displayed the works of art of Rembrandt and other Dutch masters featured in the Rijksmuseum in Amsterdam, Holland. The commentary was written in Dutch and English, and he read the English translation aloud. "You are an educated man," my mother commented.

This flattered him, and he softened and their conversation became friendly. As they spoke, he picked up a family photograph and studied it carefully. As he walked out of the room into the corridor, he noticed the grand piano. He opened the cover and fingered the piano keys.

"Would you like to play something?" Mams asked softly, and while he began to play she went into the kitchen to get some lemonade made out of home-grown lemons for the soldiers. One soldier accompanied my mother to the kitchen, no doubt to see if she was hiding anything or anybody, and returned with her as she carried in a huge tray with glasses of lemonade. The officer continued to play a piece by heart in obvious pleasure, unaware that the man he was looking for was taking a nap in the room next to the piano.

After the soldiers had finished their cold drinks, the officer ordered them to search the house. They looked under the beds, opened some armoires and large dresser drawers, opened more doors, and then came back to the living room.

"There must have been a mistake in the report than an elderly Dutch man lives on these premises. We have not seen him," the officer said, meeting my mother's eyes directly. He turned and left, taking the soldiers with him.

Mams kept her composure until the truck and car had left our driveway and were on their way down the mountain, then she began to shake uncontrollably. Our houseboy gently guided Mams to a chair and gave her some water to drink until she calmed down. Then he and Konrad moved the piano over, leaving just enough space to open the bedroom door to check on Opa, who had slept through this whole ordeal.

"You were all very brave," said Mams to us frightened children sitting on the sofa. She complimented us for sitting so quietly, for not interfering or answering questions. If the Japanese were to come back and question us children, we were to tell them that we did not know anything and had been instructed not to speak to our invaders. "There is a war going on now," my mother explained, "and the Japanese will come back. We don't want them to come, but they think they have the right to barge in any time and any day."

"But this *is* our home," I protested.

"Indeed it is," Mams softly replied, then added, "And in our home, everyone is welcome and we treat them as guests."

Chapter Five

As time went on, Opa began to slip away little by little each day. My mother called for a doctor to come; he could do nothing, he said, for Opa was dying.

Ellen and I sat down in the corridor where we could hear the commotion in Opa's bedroom. I had never before seen, nor have I since seen my mother so openly distraught. "Someone bring me the mentholatum, Opa cannot breathe. Oh please, Papa, breathe, breathe, take a deep breath . . . don't leave me now!" she cried.

Mr. Steinfurt, our big burly German neighbor—one of our few neighbors who had not been incarcerated by the Japanese—came running immediately and offered his assistance to my mother. He appeared to be trying to comfort her, and it seemed to calm her.

Konrad discovered us sitting in the corridor. He took us to Ellen's bedroom and asked us to stay in bed. "This is not a happy time and not good for little children's ears to hear," he said. "Besides, you need your beauty sleep. Why don't you girls say a little prayer for Opa and Mammy, and be good. . . ."

Ellen was scared, and I was frightened too. The concept of death had not been discussed with us. All we knew was that when people died, they were put deep in the ground in a cemetery, where it is dark and cold and lonely. We did know that the spirit would leave the body and go to heaven, but the concept of "spirit" was not really clear to us.

We decided to pray that Heavenly Father would take Opa straight to heaven to be with the angels; after all, Heavenly Father could do anything, couldn't He? Our prayer calmed us and we actually fell asleep, no longer troubled by the unknown.

We learned the next morning that Opa had passed away. We were not allowed to come out of our bedroom for a little breakfast until he was prepared for burial.

It was almost impossible to obtain a decent casket from the city. The transportation alone was very difficult, as all our vehicles had been confiscated; so we had to depend on public transportation, which was virtually non-existent. It would take too long to bring a casket up the mountain. In the tropics, unembalmed bodies are to be buried within 24 hours.

It must have been a time of deep and unbearable anguish for my mother, struggling to find a way to bury her father. The night must have been a long one for her, being alone in her grief and having the sole responsibility of arranging the funeral and the burial. I am sure that she must have prayed to Heavenly Father for comfort, solace, and insight to solve her problem.

Little did she know that the word had spread rapidly in the native *kampong*, or village, that the *Tuan Basar* had died. Despite their poverty and the extremely short notice, many of our former servants managed to provide food for the funeral.

The next morning, Mr. Steinfurt came to the house carrying a handsome homemade casket, which he and some native villagers had built together. Mr. Steinfurt was not a very sociable man and kept his distance, especially since he was German and was kept out of the camps by the Japanese because of his German citizenship. People did not trust him, nor he them. And yet, he had enough compassion to provide a casket for my grandfather's burial.

At Opa's funeral, the villagers, our friends, and former servants brought flowers and food. There was a great outpouring of love and respect. A carved headstone was even provided. Yes, Opa had a grand funeral, perfectly suited for a great man with such a big heart. Mr. Steinfurt led the funeral procession as he helped carry the casket down the mountain to the small Christian cemetery in Ambarawah, where Opa was laid to rest without any interference from the Japanese.

Chapter Six

Since my father had been in the military, he was put into a POW camp. However, he was able to escape and he eluded the Japanese for a long time. He formed a resistance force among the Indos and began to systematically destroy vital bridges, buildings, and even destroyed the machinery in his own rubber manufacturing plant—not an easy task, as that was his livelihood. For this reason, my father became a marked man; the Japanese issued a proclamation that he must be destroyed.

The effort to apprehend my father came to a head when the Japanese decided to use his family to persuade him to give himself up. My family was put under house arrest.

A huge truck came with many soldiers, who took over the house and herded us like cattle into the bedroom closest to the kitchen. There my mother gathered our little family into a circle, where we prayed for safety and for the Lord to look over us. We heard the Japanese officer in charge call to my mother to come out, but she did not until she had finished praying with us. Then, putting her finger to her mouth to remind us to remain silent, she quietly left the room. When my mother returned, her eyes looked sad and she looked very, very tired.

When we were allowed to come out, we learned that the Japanese had cemented up most of the house; we could use only a small part. We had access to one bathroom, the kitchen, the corridor, and two bedrooms, which had big windows so we could still look outside. The entrances to all other rooms were cemented up, so we could not retrieve any of our other belongings. The Japanese occupied the living quarters on the other end. But because they isolated themselves from us, we at least had our privacy.

Mams immediately took inventory of what we had and was pleased to see that the cupboards in the kitchen still held some staples and canned food. A concealed panel in the pantry next to the kitchen led to the wine cellar, and here was hidden the secret passage to the bomb shelter, which was stockpiled with food, barrels of water, medicine, extra clothes, blankets, and shoes. Mams found that the clothes hamper in the laundry room next to the bathroom was still filled with yesterday's dirty clothes and some soiled bedding, so we had a change of clothing available to us and extra sheets and pillow cases.

One door in our bedroom led to the playroom, which contained all of our toys and children's books. The Japanese had overlooked this, much to our joy and my mother's relief.

Mams instructed the boys to occupy one bedroom. By taking the mattresses off the two beds and putting them together to make one large bed, there was enough room for all three boys. The girls' room was arranged in a similar manner. Mams made her bed on a couch in the corridor.

Before retiring that evening, we had our family prayer and thanked the Lord that we were still together and that we had a good, safe place to sleep.

At dawn the next morning, we were awakened by harsh voices. We looked out of the window and saw the Japanese taking down the Dutch red, white, and blue-striped flag, which had flown from our flagpole ever since I could remember. They replaced it with the Japanese war flag, the rising sun, an indication for all to see that our property had been confiscated.

We soon learned that the Japanese had put us under house arrest to keep a close watch on us. They hoped that my father would get in touch with us and they could capture him. They also hoped to starve us into submission. However, because the bomb shelter was connected to the part of the house we occupied, my mother was able to supplement the storage in the kitchen with vegetables and soy sauce from the cache of food from the bomb shelter.

Through it all, Mams remained cheerful. She read us stories, sang songs, and played games with us little ones. When summoned for her frequent interrogations—usually by an officer who had come to inspect the premises—she was calm and collected.

One morning we were awakened by a familiar, pleasant sound. Our hearts skipped a beat when we saw several villagers passing by the house as they carried their wares to the marketplace, nonchalantly walking past the still-drowsy Japanese sentries. Their melodious tones were like love songs to our ears, spoken softly but with intensity. The women carried their baskets on their heads, and the men carried their yokes with baskets on each end, filled with their wares.

I almost shouted a greeting to them, but Mams gently placed a hand over my mouth, and with the other put her finger to her lips to indicate the need for silence. As we stood listening to the voices, a smile came over her face and tears flowed down her cheeks. The villagers appeared to be talking among themselves and did not appear to even notice us standing at the window. One villager, however, looked up as if to gaze at the rising sun and caught my mother's eyes. They shared a smile, and Mams put the fingers of both her hands together and bowed her head slightly, returning the greeting in their familiar fashion. But to one who knew their native dialect, their words communicated to my mother, their *Nonya Manis*, their Sweet Lady. While my mother understood and spoke the local dialect, the Japanese did not.

The chief and elders of the village had suggested that the villagers blaze a new trail to the marketplace, one that went through our property and beside the house. This action would actually save them time because it was a shorter way than taking the main road, and they would have a logical explanation should the Japanese protest.

Our father was safe, was their message, and he was nearby. They indicated also that they would pass by the next day and would throw a stone, with a message from my father wrapped around it, through the window. When my mother had a message for my dad, she should throw the same stone out of the window by night, and they would look for it as they passed by the house the next day.

Because my parents had insisted on educating the young people in the village, they were able to help us and more than willing to do so. Those who had learned to read and write would send us the messages. It was a tricky business, and if they were caught it could cost them their lives. Yet they were willing to do it for us.

These messages kept us in touch with what was going on around us in the world, prepared us for what might be our lot, and eventually saved our lives.

As the days went by, the villagers became bolder and bolder, the women flirting openly with the sentries as the men threw us packages that contained beef, chicken, or fish, which we sorely needed. My mother thanked Heavenly Father fervently for the loyalty and love these villagers extended to us—and thanked him as well for sending us three of the most stupid sentries in the Japanese army to guard us. They never noticed that we had a food storage on hand, nor did they ever see the packages flying through the windows!

While under this house arrest, my mother, who had been pregnant when the Japanese took over our house, gave birth to my youngest brother. She had prepared herself well for this event, and had even boiled the water beforehand. When we were awakened by a newborn baby's cry, we knew that our little baby was born. My sister Annalise had assisted my mother and was proudly beaming from ear to ear. My new little brother was given the name Dieudonne William (which meant "Given by God"). We called him Wim.

The Japanese sentries were amazed that my mother had given birth to this little baby boy alone, and so quietly. Perhaps because they were fathers themselves, or perhaps because tender feelings came into their hearts (babies have a tendency to evoke these feelings), they became very solicitous about my mother's well-being, even offering their services to her. My mother asked them to bring her the baby clothes and especially the baby diapers and pins from the nursery next to the master bedroom, which the Japanese sentries now occupied. They brought all the baby things to her, from crib to diaper pail. Gratefully and with tears brimming in her eyes, my mother sank to her knees to thank them for their generosity. After that, my mother was able to extract special favors from one of the soldiers. He brought in her sewing basket and her sewing machine, and she mended his uniform for him.

When my father learned that his family had been taken prisoners, he sent a message to my mother that he would surrender in exchange for our freedom. "Stay in hiding," was the message she sent back. She knew promises would be broken, and we would be incarcerated. Nevertheless, she prepared us for this eventuality.

Using pillow cases, she sewed backpacks for each of us children and herself. The backpacks even had handles on them so we could carry them on our backs. She packed them with dried fruit, dried meat similar to jerky, a hand towel, a toothbrush, a comb, and soap, as well as a set of clean underwear and outer clothing made out of the sturdiest material she could find. Mams also placed our favorite toy next to our backpacks on a chair.

Because she was a pharmacist, she had stored medicine in the bomb shelter and was able to color-code it to our level of understanding so that we could use it when we needed it. The quinine pills, for example, were red because quinine is used to combat malaria, which can be contracted from a mosquito who sucks contaminated blood and then transmits the disease through your blood. Blood is red, so quinine was the red pill.

The white tablets were chlorine to purify drinking water. White is the color for purity, so we used the white tablets. She impressed upon our minds the importance of drinking only pure water.

The color of death is black, and the black pills were to fight against the bacteria that causes cholera. Cholera is spread through polluted water, contaminated food, or insects; the disease causes sudden onset of severe vomiting and diarrhea. Left untreated, the resulting dehydration is often fatal. Today, we fight cholera through inoculation.

The bright yellow pills were vitamins, which bring vitality to your body just as the sun brings brightness and vitality to all living things on the earth. This pill would make us feel better.

Because Mams' new baby was a male child, she was not sure whether the Japanese would allow her to take him with her; so she placed small bands on her new baby's ankles and wrists. The bands read "Dieudonne, son of Anna Johannes," and his birth date. If she had to give him up, at least someone would be able to identify him.

All of our clothing was clearly identified with our names in case we were separated. Small children separated from their parents or siblings, upon finding themselves alone in a strange concentration camp, could become so traumatized that they would actually forget their own names. Children who died would be buried without any identification. She did not want this to happen to us.

And so, prepared for whatever the future would bring, we waited.

Chapter Seven

It was on a rainy day, when the water seemed to pour out of the heavens in buckets, that we received the news that my father had been captured. It would now be only a matter of time to hear what punishment awaited him. My mother was tense and jittery as she waited for news from the villagers—any news, good or bad.

One day Daniel spotted a military car coming up the mountain in our direction. Mams gathered us for prayer to ask Heavenly Father to calm our nerves and quiet her pounding heart, to protect and to strengthen our dad, and to give him fortitude to bear all things that lay ahead of him. She thanked God for having protected my father and us so long from harm and unpleasantness. Then she asked God to bless his captors that they would be merciful. We all cried during this prayer. We were terrified for our father's safety.

Just as we were finishing our prayer, a Japanese officer came into our quarters—the same officer who had previously come to the house to search for Opa. He stood at the door for a moment, his face solemn. My mother motioned us to sit down together on the floor, which we quietly did. Konrad held the baby in his arms, slowly rocking him back and forth to keep him from crying. My mother walked towards the visitor, bowed, and greeted him as if he were an honored guest instead of our captor.

"I must inform you, madam, that your husband has been captured and is incarcerated," he said. "He is a most dangerous man to the Japanese Empire and will be punished severely for his resistance actions and for the destruction he has caused."

My mother gave no indication that she already knew this,

because of the messages from the faithful villagers. "Where has he been taken?" she asked quietly.

"He has been detained in Ambarawah for now, but he will be transferred to a more suitable camp at a later time" was the answer. He was not at liberty to give more information.

My mother's hands began to shake and her eyes filled with tears. "Thank you for bringing me this information," she said to the officer and bowed her head.

The officer looked uncomfortable at what he was forced to say next. "I regret to inform you," he said, "You must come with me."

At Mother's quick look towards her children, he shook his head. "Your children must stay here. You must quickly pack what you will need for a few days."

My mother protested. She pointed to her new baby and asked if she could take him, as she needed to nurse him to keep him alive. The Japanese officer paused for a moment, then nodded his head. Mams quickly packed a few diapers in her backpack and wrapped the baby in a blanket, totally covering him with it to protect him from the driving rain. Then she kissed each of us, whispering a few soft words of comfort to each of us. Ellen and I began to cry, and when Mams turned to leave, we began to cry even louder. Her face torn with anguish, she ran back to hug us one more time.

A chill came into the room and we were all cold, so Konrad closed the bedroom windows and suggested that we go to bed early. He took a book from the stack we kept in the hall and curled up on the floor against the couch where my mother usually slept. Herbert also found a book and curled up on the couch itself to read, resting his head on Mams' pillow. Daniel invited me to play a board game with him, but I shook my head numbly. So he played by himself, throwing the dice forcefully and moving the pieces noisily up and down on the board.

I huddled in a corner of the room, my back pressed against the wall, holding a pillow against my face so no one would hear me cry.

Ellen sucked her thumb and walked dazedly back and forth. Whimpering and crying softly, she took deep breaths and her body shuddered. Konrad called her to come and sit with him and she cuddled up against him. After a while she fell asleep in his arms, exhausted. Annalise stayed by the closed window, looking out into the darkened sky. She was deep in thought. After a little while she went into the kitchen to fix us some soup, which warmed us and took the chill out of our bodies.

At about 8 o'clock, two sentries came in to check up on us. It was very dark outside and we were allowed to have only one small light, which was in the corridor near my mother's sleeping area, where the boys were reading. The sentries pounded on the door before opening it, and I began to scream and could not stop. One sentry hollered for me to be quiet, and the other turned on the light, which made me stop screaming.

He turned to Konrad and said that we could leave one other light on during the night. The other guard left and returned with blankets taken from the other bedrooms or from the guest homes. We did not care where they came from; we were just glad to have them, because it grew so very cold in the mountains.

Meanwhile, the first guard walked into the kitchen and asked Annalise if we had something to eat. She told him we had some soup. Then they both left, locking the big door with a key.

Because our mother had forbidden us to have any conversation with our guards, we really did not know their real names; so we gave each of them a nickname. Guard number one was "Mr. Bigbelly," the second was "Mr. Mustache," and the third was "Mr. Sleepy."

Konrad took the lead and said the evenings prayers by reciting the Lord's prayer—with an additional petition for the safety of our father and mother—before we all went to sleep.

Near dawn, the villagers came by the house again on their way to the marketplace. It had stopped raining, but the ground was still wet and muddy in some places. The villagers asked where our mother was, as she was not at her regular place. They told us to write a message and throw it in the rocks, and they would find it on their way back from the market. Konrad took a paper and wrote that our mother had been taken away, then he wrapped it around a rock, tied it, and tossed it out the window among the rocks.

That day was a lonely one. We took turns at the window, watching hopefully for the return of our mother. Herbert saw that the rock with the message was picked up by one of our former gardeners, who had looked up at him and waved.

By evening it started to rain again, and we were discouraged and hungry. We knew there was food in the bomb shelter, but we were afraid that we might in some way reveal it to our captors.

Suddenly Daniel had an idea. "There's food in our backpacks! We can use it now and replace it when Mams comes back."

"What if we need it later?" Konrad asked hesitantly.

"But we need it now," Daniel said firmly. And Konrad reluctantly agreed.

We had just finished eating our fruit when the sentries came in with a large bowl of white rice, dried fish, and a plate with steaming hot vegetables. We could not believe our eyes! Annalise dished out the food, leaving half of it for us to use the next day, but the sentry, whom we had nicknamed "Mr. Bigbelly," motioned for us to eat all of it. "Tomorrow you will get more! Don't worry," he said. He did not have to say more.

That evening, Annalise took the lead in our family prayer. She thanked our Heavenly Father for the food and blankets that we had received, and then beseeched Him to watch over and protect our father and mother. Afterwards we sang "Abide with Me, 'Tis Eventide."

On the second day of our mother's absence, the villagers left us a package of wonderful treats. They certainly remembered what kind of food would cheer up children!

About midday, a military car came up the mountain road. We waited impatiently until we saw my mother's arm waving a baby's diaper to us. We joined hands and danced around the room. "Mams is back, Mams is back!!" we all sang.

She stepped out of the car with the baby in one arm and her backpack in the other. She looked tired, as if she had not slept at all during her absence. Her eyes were sunken deep into their sockets and she had large, dark-colored rings around her eyes. When the sentries opened the door to let her into the house, she smiled tiredly at us. She handed the baby to Annalise with a hug and then opened her arms wide to gather in Ellen and me. She spoke quietly to each of her children, then lay down on her couch and closed her eyes. Herbert propped a pillow behind her head to make her comfortable while Annalise took the baby, washed and changed him and fed him some ricewater. We were all very quiet, but our hearts rejoiced because Mammy was back.

Chapter Eight

We learned that Mams had been driven to Ambarawah, where they stopped briefly before heading on to the city of Semarang, the capitol of mid-Java. The town bank had been converted into the military headquarters, and there she was told to wait in a long line that did not move. The people were forbidden to speak with one another and so stood silent, although a few spoke in nervous whispers.

She was terribly thirsty, and it was hot and stuffy in the hall where she waited. Fortunately, the baby continued to sleep, as he had during most of the drive. The hours ticked away without answers, and she lay on the cool, tiled floor and tried to rest herself for what was ahead.

Her name was finally called the next day, and she was motioned to follow an Indonesian who apparently worked for the Japanese. She walked down endless hallways, wondering how she would ever find her way out. She shuddered at the thought that she might have to walk home. She began to feel faint. At last she spoke.

"I am so very thirsty and I haven't eaten for two days. Could we please not walk so fast?"

The clerk slowed his steps and asked, "Are you related in any way to the Johan van Burg who used to have a sausage factory in Batu?"

"Yes, that was my father," she replied. "He passed away three months ago. Did you know him?"

"Oh, yes," the clerk smiled. "I used to work for him. He was a very fair man."

After that they walked in silence, the clerk having slowed his pace considerably. At last he paused beside a door and waved my mother into the room. "Sit," he said, pointing toward a chair and desk. He also indicated a private rest room where she could refresh herself, then left her alone, closing the door behind him. Mother wondered what would be next.

She was surprised and thankful when he returned with a large pitcher of iced tea, which he poured into a glass for her. He then took some food from another tray. Too tired to eat, she drank only the iced tea.

"You must eat," he insisted, and he waited patiently until she had done so.

After she had eaten, he opened a manila folder which contained papers about my mother and her family. "What is this all about?" she asked.

"The Japanese need to interrogate you," he replied. "Have you regained your strength? Are you ready?" She asked for time to nurse and change the baby, and he allowed her time to do so.

After she had rested a little longer, the clerk took her to another part of the building, where, again, she was ordered to wait. This time, however, the baby started to cry, and she tried to calm him by rocking him back and forth. "Oh, Heavenly Father, let this pass," she silently prayed. "Let me be allowed to go back to the children at home."

Her name was called. Two Japanese guards took her into a room, where she was pushed down on a chair. The baby started crying, and she put him on the floor on the blanket right next to her. Soon he fell asleep again.

A high-ranking Japanese officer with glasses and a moustache asked her question after question, sometimes the same one over and over again. Did she know that her husband had escaped and was involved in a resistance force? What did she know about this organization? Could she mention names of people involved in this? She did not know them, she said. At last he let her go.

Before Mams left the room, she asked the officer if he knew where my father was. "How is he?" she pleaded. The question took him aback. He studied her face, then gave orders in Japanese to the guards, who opened another door. The officer motioned my mother to go inside the other room, which was hot and airless and smelled of sweat and urine.

There in the dimly lit room sat my father, tied to a chair, his face bleeding and swollen from beatings. How glad she was that she had not attempted to give names of any possible members of the resistance! The officer watched her closely as she took a diaper from her bag and gently cleaned my father's face. Then she walked back to the room where she had been interrogated and took a glass of water from the table, which she gave to my father to drink. No word was spoken between them, but their eyes communicated their love and pride, and offered encouragement to go on. When my mother bent to kiss my father, the officer turned his head as if to give them a moment of privacy.

Too soon the officer barked a command in Japanese. My father's hands were loosened, and he was taken away. "Goodbye, Anneke," my father managed to whisper.

"Not goodbye," said my mother, "but until we meet again. Take courage."

She did not remember walking through the maze of halls and doors in that building. Outside it was dark. She had no money, no food or water, and no place to sleep. She decided to walk as far as possible in the direction of Ambarawah to try to get home to us. As she walked she prayed to Heavenly Father and thanked Him for allowing her to see her husband. She prayed for his safety, as it was known that people had been executed for lesser crimes than sabotage. Suddenly she realized that she had not shown him their new baby. This was too much for her, and she began to cry.

She walked most of the night, pausing under a railroad bridge after someone warned her that a curfew was in place. Additionally, it had begun to rain. It was nearly impossible to walk in the pitch dark night.

At dawn, she was well on her way on the road to Ambarawah when a military car overtook her, stopped, then backed up and stopped right next to her. "Oh, no, not again," she gasped.

"Mrs. Anna, come into the car," a familiar voice called out. She looked into the car and recognized the same Japanese officer who had taken her away. She opened the front door and sat down next to the driver. No questions were asked, no one spoke. My mother closed her eyes and slept until they reached our little village. As she looked up at the house, filled with gratitude that she was going home, she noticed

Daniel half-hanging out the window and could not resist waving at him with the baby's diaper.

That night our sentries again gave us a good meal. Our evening prayers were jubilant, and we gratefully thanked our Heavenly Father for our many blessings, acknowledging His hand in all things. We petitioned the Lord to watch over and protect our father and to bless him with courage and strength to bear his difficulties. Mams must have worried about my father's condition, but she never let us see her sorrow.

Chapter Nine

My mother was not able to rest for long after her ordeal. Only a few days later, the Japanese came to take all of us to a concentration camp.

My mother had been prepared and waiting for them to do just this, and had replenished our backpacks with dried food from the shelter. She and Annalise had also packed two large suitcases with our clothes and other belongings. The Japanese soldiers came very early in the morning, and I was too sleepy to think clearly; consequently I left my favorite toy—Pop Mientje, my rag doll—behind. Mams had given me instructions to be in charge of her black bag, and in my haste I had grabbed my backpack and the black bag, but left my rag doll behind.

Our regular sentries—"Mr. Bigbelly," "Mr. Mustache," and "Mr. Sleep"—stood together silently on the side of the house while others took over. Mams approached the one in charge and said, "We have not yet had the chance to say our morning prayers. It would be most beneficial to the boys to receive a blessing from God." They gave their permission and we were allowed to have this last family prayer, in which my mother invoked the Lord's choices blessings to be with her boys and to protect them.

"Bless our captors, dear Lord, and soften their hearts so they will use mercy and kindness as they deal with our family," she continued. And then she asked a blessing on each of her sons. First, on Herbie, who could not comprehend and was perplexed by the cruelty and vindictiveness of war. "Bless Herbie," she prayed. "He has always been a peaceful young man. Bless him that his mind will be at ease."

There was also a blessing of faith and fortitude for Konrad, and

Daniel was cautioned not to provoke but to be prudent. "Take courage, my boys," she said. "Remember that you are the sons of God and your father's offspring. Be proud of your heritage!" She reminded them to remember her teachings for survival, and to guard their backpacks and the articles in them. Later, Mams told us that she had been able to put a bag of salt and money in each of the boys' backpacks—as people in camps would sell their food for money and even the native Indonesians would provide food for money or barter for salt.

Saying goodbye to one another was difficult, because we realized that we might never see each other again. It was especially heartbreaking for my mother. As a mother, she knew her children's weaknesses and their strengths, and she knew their chances of survival. Bravely she embraced and kissed her sons, and whispered softly to each of them special words intended only for their ears.

Konrad and Daniel were put in a small truck together. Daniel, with tears running down his face, stretched his arms out toward his mother. Konrad put his arm around him and waved bravely at Mams, as if to tell her not to worry. Herbie was placed in a second vehicle, and as the car moved away, Herbie never took his eyes from my mother. As the car moved out of sight, my mother saw him hold up his hand high above his head in a final farewell. That glimpse of his hand was the last she saw of him. For the next three years, my mother would worry especially about Herbie, knowing that he did not have his family near him to provide the emotional support he would need, especially during such difficult times.

My mother, the baby, my sisters, and myself were led to yet a third truck. The baby happened to be dressed in pink that day, so his gender was not questioned and he was sent along with my mother. For the first few days we even called him "Wilhelmina" instead of Wim. Ellen and I thought it was just wonderful to have a little baby "sister" to play with and to fuss over!

As we were driven slowly through the village in the open truck, many of our neighbors and friends could see us, and they waved. We could see some of our former servants, many of them crying when they noticed us. We saw Baboe Kit and our faithful houseboy, Resoh, at a distance. They courteously bowed their heads and waved at us. My mother acknowledged their greeting, then slowly turned back to the road in the direction where the boys had gone. Observing all the loving people of the village who had gathered to pay final homage to their Nonya Manis, my mother looked about her, as if taking a photograph of this scene. In this way, she said goodbye to her beautiful house, her friends, and to the good life she had known.

We were taken to a concentration camp, where we encountered friends we did not recognize because of the changes that had come over them through hunger and disease. It was hot and humid, and the stench was horrible. Our barracks were infested with flies, lice, roaches, rats, and mosquitoes.

We were each allowed one and a half meters of space on the dirt floor on which to sleep. Because we had brought blankets with us, we did not have to sleep on the dirty mats that were provided for us. After we had been assigned our spot, Mams saw an older woman lying asleep in a corner on the damp dirt floor. She had nothing to lie on.

"Ellen, Kitty," Mams turned to us, "would you share a blanket, so this woman need not lie in the dirt?" She then walked over to the old woman and offered her our blanket. The woman was too ill or too weak to respond, so Mams picked her up and gently arranged the blanket beneath her.

Then our mother arranged our little area. Instead of having us sleep next to one another in a row, she arranged it so that she would sleep lengthwise in the middle of our spot, and our heads would touch her sides. Closest to her heart were the baby and Ellen, because they were the youngest. Annalise and I were closer to her feet. Mams explained that she wanted to be able to have us within her reach when she wanted to touch us. "I only have to stretch out my arms to find you," she said.

We, of course, benefited more from this arrangement than Mams did. When it was dark and frightening with all these strange noises, in this unfamiliar place amidst all these people, it was so comforting to feel our mother so close by—to feel her warmth and often her soft caress on our heads or on our arms. She was even able to fashion our mosquito nets over our sleeping area with poles driven into the ground to protect us from the ever-troublesome mosquitoes.

While in this camp, we continued to have prayer each morning to thank Heavenly Father for food and water, and for our lives. Since it was forbidden to display any form of religion, we had to get up very early in order to be able to kneel and say our prayers. Always we asked the Lord to watch over the boys and my father, and to sustain them in their hour of need.

"Why are you so foolish to risk your lives to pray to a God who does not seem to hear us or care about us?" our prisonmates asked us. "If He cared, would we be in this terrible place?"

My mother calmly ignored the disparaging remarks of others and continued to teach us of peaceable things. She had no Bible, but her memory of its teachings was phenomenal. Each morning after prayers, Mams reminded us that we were to "love your enemies, bless them that curse you, do good to them that hate you, and pray for them that despitefully use you and persecute you; That ye may be the children of your Father, which is in heaven: for he maketh the sun to rise on the evil and the good, and sendeth rain on the just and on the unjust." (Matt. 5:44-45.) How she knew her scriptures and was able to derive great strength from them in her hours of need!

She also taught us that because we were fed little food and water, our energy level would be very low. If we were to use this little energy that we had to hate our enemies, to hate our environment, and to hate the people around us, that hate would consume this little energy needlessly and get us nowhere. But if we were to use this little energy to love our God first and to love those around us, or at least to see the good in them, love would enhance our character; and "with this love we can shame our oppressors by proving that we are better human beings" (Mahatma Gandhi).

The women had to work during the day, so we children were mostly left on our own. With nothing to do, many became restless and bored. Ofttimes the older ones resorted to mischief to keep themselves occupied; some even stooped to stealing from one other, as their mothers were not there to chastise or correct them.

Ellen and I kept to ourselves most of the time and seldom interacted with the Dutch children. We were the only Indo children in this particular camp and a racial barrier had always existed between the Dutch and the Indos, although as children we were unaware of this in our sheltered mountain home. Our friends at home had been other Indo children, Javanese children, or the children of our Dutch friends whom we had known most of our lives. Most of the Dutch children were from the city where they had gone to school together, and they never invited us to join in their games or frolicking. We were not accustomed to the ways of the blonde Dutch children, so we kept our distance and amused ourselves in our own quiet way.

Our mother, however, would draw the camp children around her for Bible storytelling, especially when atrocities were committed by the Japanese and we were forced to watch them. To shield us from the atrocities committed by the soldiers upon the prisoners, she would place herself in front of us and say, "I think that you children would prefer to hear a story about Jesus, rather than watching these awful things." Then she would sit down on the ground and begin to tell the stories. Many other children would sit down with us and listen, fascinated.

I can still see my mother walking around the camp with the baby swaddled in a *slendang*, a rectangular piece of cloth holding the baby against her body and fastened at one shoulder with a big knot. This left her arms free to do her required work while still carrying little Wim close to her heart.

My mother taught us by example to live a pure and Christian life amidst the suffering and injustices that we saw and experienced. But she also had great courage to bear the consequences of her own actions, because she would not compromise her beliefs in the teachings of Christ.

Chapter Ten

As my mother had been appointed our barracks spokesperson, one day it fell upon her shoulders to provide twenty-eight young women between the ages of fourteen and twenty-two to be used as prostitutes for the Japanese officers, who were celebrating a holiday. She could not take it upon herself to choose which of the girls were to be submitted to this humiliating indignity. And so she took this problem to the Lord.

She fasted and prayed, and we believe that she was inspired to shave off all the hair of some sixty young women in that age group. Because her black medical bag had not been taken from her, she was able to use the scissors, razor blades, sharp medical instruments, and the two hair clippers from her bag.

To prevent the Japanese from discovering her plan until the very last moment, she had to wait until after work detail had been completed. This meant that she had exactly three and a half minutes to do all of this, since this was how long it would take for the Japanese officers to walk from their upper barracks to ours, if they did so at a leisurely pace. Although Mams asked for volunteers to help her, only six mothers dared to come forward to help her save their daughters.

Mams also passed among the girls some pieces of a very poisonous plant she had found growing near the barbed wire fence and encouraged the girls to smear the sap all over their bodies. Because of her knowledge of herbs and plants, she knew that this sap would give off a noxious odor, which would make them doubly unappealing to the Japanese officers. Since the plant was so poisonous, she cautioned the girls not to rub it on their bodies if they had the slightest cut.

At the appointed time, there stood some sixty foul-smelling girls with shaven heads waiting for the Japanese officers who had come to claim their prizes. Punishment for the guilty was inevitable, as this was considered an open revolt.

Everyone was ordered to gather outside the barracks; even the sick people had to leave their sickbeds and stand in military ranks for roll call. The Japanese officers loved to count their prisoners and purposely took their time as we stood in the hot sun. We were refused water or latrine privileges, and many fainted as we stood there in the tropical heat and listened as a furious Japanese officer screamed at us. We were "nothing," he said. All power was held by the Japanese Imperial Armed Forces. We were now subject to the Japanese Emperor, and he could do anything he wanted with us. We would never be free.

The officers took turns screaming insults at us and slapping the women. At last they took my mother and the six mothers who had helped her and stood them before the other women. Then they ripped their clothing off their bodies and ridiculed and shamed them. It was a horrible scene.

One officer pointed to my mother. "Why have you done this wrong against the officers of the Japanese Imperial Forces?" he demanded. "You have been appointed to be a barracks unit leader. You must set an example of obedience." He made a mistake by placing a bullhorn against her mouth for her response, and she took the opportunity to testify how she had found the courage for what she had done.

"My God has sanctified some things in our lives," she said. "Virtue is one of these. As a Christian people, we have been commanded to live virtuous lives. Violations of the law of chastity are grievous sins in the eyes of my God, whether they be permitted by us or committed by others such as you. We will protect this virtue at all costs, even unto death. As one of the leaders here, I will take responsibility for the action that I have taken."

This infuriated the Japanese, who slapped my mother about the face until blood flowed from her nose and mouth. Then they bound her against a pole with her hands over her head so that she would be completely defenseless.

"So you are a Christian," they asked her. "Are you willing to die for this cause?"

"I am," she answered. Again they slapped her as they continued to ask questions that were blasphemous to her ears, and from that point on she refused to answer.

A samurai sword was drawn, and as we had witnessed frequent beheadings before, we thought she surely would be beheaded. Instead, the man used the sword to cut a cross on her bare back. A samurai sword is razor-sharp, but its victim does not bleed right away. Its cuts are nonetheless deep and painful. The Japanese prided themselves on sharpening their swords and bayonets in front of us every day.

The officer nicked my mother a few times on her arms, causing the blood to flow. The beatings began again, this time with belts. The buckle of one belt became stuck where the two cuts of the cross met, ripping a piece of flesh from my mother's back. My sweet mother remained silent, although tears streamed down her face, mingling with her blood.

When at last the officers cut her loose, she lost her balance and fell. As she slowly got to her knees, one officer kicked her in the belly and she fell backwards. Again she got to her knees, and then to her feet, where she stood erect, her head high. The Japanese were visibly annoyed; they had expected her to stand with her head bowed, a sign of shame and defeat.

The officers dismissed the other women and focused on my mother, who had been the "ringleader." As punishment, she was sentenced to two weeks in the pit.

The "pits" were holes in the ground, about seven or eight feet deep, where one could stand or squat, but never lie down, because the pits were not wide enough. The tops were covered with chicken wire and fastened on all sides. Food and water was thrown into the pit. One had to stand in one's own filth, reduced to a state below that of a caged animal, as at least animal cages were cleaned periodically. Usually those sentenced to the pit did not survive because of the physical, emotional, and psychological torture.

The sentence was pronounced, and my mother's eyes sought her children in the multitude and beckoned us to come to her. Even in her pain she remembered to show respect for the customs of her captors, using her whole arm to summon us instead of using only the two fingers of her hand, as this latter gesture was very offensive to the Orientals. We ran towards her immediately. One woman stopped Annalise and gave her a piece of cloth to give to our mother to wipe the blood from her face and body and to cover, at least in part, her nakedness.

Mams bent down to our level and looked each of us in the eyes. Her eyes were tearless as she asked us to remain faithful and to sustain her with our prayers. "Now, I need you children to be brave and to continue to get up early in the morning to pray to our Heavenly Father daily," she said. "Thank Him for the blessings of life. Ask Him to continue to bless you, to watch over you and to keep you safe. Then ask Him to have mercy on me and to bless me with inner strength, so that I may survive this ordeal and come back to you and continue to be your mother here on earth until you are old enough to take care of yourselves."

Before we could kiss her or say goodbye, she was led away. Because she was covered in blood, the soldiers did not lead her roughly by the arms as they usually did, and she was free to turn around to give us a final, parting message. She said simply, "Children, remember the garden in Gethsemane!"

How well we remembered the story of the garden in Gethsemane, where our dear Savior, Jesus Christ, asked his very best friends to watch and pray as he went through agonizing pain, taking upon himself all the sins of this world. But instead, they had fallen asleep. Three times our Savior found them asleep, and to Peter he said finally, "Could ye not watch with me one hour?" (Matthew 26:40.)

This was *not* going to happen to our mother! We would watch and pray. Each day we fervently prayed for our mother's well-being, as well as for our father and brothers as we continued to defy orders not to hold any religious activities.

The first night alone in the camp without our mother was a frightening experience. We rearranged ourselves in our sleeping area; Annalise took my mother's place, with the baby and Ellen on each side of her. As the second oldest daughter, I acted as the other "guardian" and slept at the other end.

Without our mother to care for us, obtaining food was a

problem. Annalise fiercely defended our position when standing in line to receive our food, determined to take care of us all by herself. She wisely gave me more responsibility and placed me "in charge" of Ellen. I was to make sure that Ellen ate her food, and I was to take her to the latrine. Since Ellen and I were always together, this left me little time to explore and wander. Although I felt very important to be in charge of these duties, I missed the loving nurturing of my mother. There was no peace in our hearts, just fear and anxiety.

Through the grace of the Lord, my mother survived her ordeal. It was a tremendously happy moment when we heard the shouting that my mother was released and saw her walk slowly towards us, her arms open to us, inviting us to come to her. Someone had given her a sheet to cover her nakedness, and it felt good to feel her warmth through it as she embraced us.

Mams took the time to greet the many women who came forward to welcome her, yet as I watched I knew that she must have been in great pain. Her legs and feet were swollen to at least three times their normal size, and she looked utterly exhausted. Her lips were blistered and her eyes swollen from being exposed to the elements for such a long period of time.

Mams was led towards our barracks and into the washing area, where it was discovered that her body had already begun to rot. We took many live maggots from her bare back and lovingly washed her with water collected by the women in the barracks, who had sacrificed their washing water for her.

Water was a very precious commodity, as we were allowed only one small basin of washing water each day. Many of the women suffered from diseases and needed the water to quench their thirst, to keep their fever down, or just to wash their bodies and clothes. Yet these women had sacrificed their washing water to bathe my mother.

After Mams was washed and dressed in clean clothes, her first act was to go on her knees, in the open for everyone to see, defying the prohibition of any expression of religion. She was especially thankful to Heavenly Father for preserving her life by sending rain. It had rained three times during this usually dry season, and she was able to collect clean water by scraping dirt down from the wall of her pit to create a shelf for her drinking cup to stand on. In this manner she could catch this rainwater so that it would not mingle with the filth in the bottom of the pit.

She was also able to catch pieces of food and water with her open mouth as it was thrown into the pit each day, without wasting too much. At mid-day a breeze would come, moving branches from a nearby tree to shade her, giving her some relief from the hot tropical sun. To us this was a manifestation that there was indeed a Heavenly Father who was mindful of our plight, who had heard our petitions and had shown mercy by answering our prayers and sending our mother back to us.

That same afternoon we had to stand in line to receive our food and water rations. Our mother could barely stand, let alone walk, but she knew she needed nourishment. So she stood in line with us, in obvious pain, leaning heavily on a stick. Seeing my mother like that fueled the hatred in my heart for those responsible, and I forgot my mother's teachings and lost control. When I passed one of the officers who handled our rations, I threw my cup of precious drinking water in his face and spat at him. Then I said the most unkind words I could think of.

Immediately a samurai sword was drawn toward me. Quickly my mother put her hands on the sword and pushed it away from me, cutting her hands in the process.

"Please pick up your cup, Kitty, and apologize," she begged me softly. But I stood there frozen with fear. I knew that when a soldier draws a samurai sword, he will use it—and I feared the worst.

In those moments, my mother taught me the true virtue of charity. She became my mediator, as Jesus Christ is for each of us. With great difficulty she bent and picked up the cup, then bowed deeply, as was required when addressing the Japanese. She offered apologies in my name, explaining that I was only a child and had not acquired the discipline to master my emotions, and she asked the Japanese officer to please have mercy on me. "If there must be a punishment," she said, "I will take it for my child."

After a long, searching look at my mother, the officer slowly put the sword back in its sheath, gently took the cup from my mother's hands and filled it with water. "Woman, drink!" he said, and surprised but grateful, my mother drank the water. He took the cup from her hands, filled it a second time, and again offered it to my mother with both hands and a slight bow, which is a sign of respect.

"It is I who must apologize to you for not recognizing the majesty of your womanhood," he said. Her courageous interference had awakened in him the realization that this war had made a savage out of him. He had always considered himself an honorable man— until now, when he was about to lower himself to strike and hurt a child. "Thank you," he said, "for reminding me of my honorable manhood. I am now able to return to my very own family in Japan after this war, a much better man. *Domo arigato!"*

My mother bent her head toward him. "Truly, you have the spirit of *Ishido* in you!" she reciprocated. The spirit of *Ishido* means a "warrior with great wisdom," which is the highest compliment one can give to a Japanese warrior. In this my mother showed us that she was wise, and also that she was educated, because she knew about different cultures and could reciprocate appropriately. She also had a special ability to bring out the best in people.

Gratitude welled up in my heart at my mother's love. Truly she taught us to "love your enemies, and do good, and lend, hoping for nothing again; and your reward shall be great, and ye shall be the children of the Highest: for he is kind unto the unthankful and to the evil." (Luke 6:35.)

Chapter Eleven

We had been in the camp about three months when I had my ninth birthday and received an unexpected visitor. I had wandered away from the barracks in search of fresh air and was just standing at the outskirts of the compound looking around me when I thought I heard my name called, "Kitty, Kitty," then softly, "*Ittepetit!*"

I immediately knew that it was my nanny calling me, because that was the nickname she had given me. Looking around anxiously, I finally saw her, sitting and waiting patiently in the underbrush and smiling at me.

"Oh, Baboe Kit, have you come to take me away from this awful place?" I asked.

"No, my child," came the familiar voice. "I have come to give you something because today is your birthday!"

Pretending that I was playing with my stick in case any Japanese soldiers should see me, I came closer to her. "Baboe Kit," I pleaded, "please, take me with you. I hate it here."

"Shh. . . .," she admonished me sternly. "You must keep your voice down. Now listen to what I have to say. I have walked a great distance and waited here at the gate for many days to see you. I have here your rag doll. You left her behind when you were taken, and she wants to be here in this camp with you." She told me that native nannies were not allowed in the camp and that it was very dangerous for European children to live in the village, especially for someone as tall as I was.

"Remember to say your prayers," she continued, "to ask for strength and endurance, and to be obedient, and Allah's spirit will be with you and protect you. This, too, shall pass, God willing. Perhaps there is a purpose for which you need to go through these bad times. Remember, there is to be opposition in all things, to have to taste of the bitter to savor the sweet things in life, to be hungry to appreciate an abundance of food, to be held captive to cherish and protect freedom. Remember to be obedient, and Allah will be with you.

"I know that it is *not* your destiny to die in this concentration camp. Take this doll, protect her, and she will bring you comfort. Now, swear on Allah's holy name that you will take care of this doll." She told me to turn towards the holy city of Mecca and swear that I would take care of this doll.

So I shifted my position, then crawled closer to the barbed wire. I had learned to be obedient to my nanny at all times, but this time the need for her touch was too great. When she handed me the doll our hands touched and she stroked my hand. Again, I pleaded, "Oh, please, Nanny, take me with you!" and threw the doll aside, reaching out for her with both hands and cutting my face on the barbed wire as I attempted to press my body closer to her. I could smell her familiar fragrance. I closed my eyes, savoring the seconds of feeling her arms around me and her soft hands caressing my face, wiping away my tears.

She whispered a few endearing words into my ears, then suddenly and urgently said, "I must go now. Go quickly and take your doll!"

She pulled back from me, but I could not let her go, did not want to let her go. I could not see, as she did, the sentry who was coming toward us. As I held onto Nanny for one last second, trying to kiss her one more time, the sentry saw us. Thinking that she was escaping from the camp, he took aim and fired.

A gaping, bloody wound appeared in my nanny's back. She turned around to face me, clasped her hands in front of her in a final bow, and smiled at me as if to tell me that it was all right before she fell to the ground.

In the confusion of shouting sentries and screaming women that followed the shooting, no one paid attention as I stood there in shock, watching my nanny die, hearing her cry, thinking, *Why did there have to be opposition in all things? Why was life so horrible and so unfair? Why did I have to stand there helpless, separated from my nanny by the barbed wire fence?*

It was of course my mother who found me, clutching my doll against me. Instantly she knew that I had seen my nanny, and she folded me into her arms as she gently led me away from the spot and explained to me, "Nanny must have known that she would be risking her life to come to see her darling child here, but nevertheless she came because she loved you. She knew that you missed your rag doll and wanted to bring her to you."

Then I understood the true meaning of the Bible scripture that said, "Greater love hath no man than this, that a man lay down his life for his friends." (John 15:13.)

"We need to remember the good things about Baboe Kit," my mother continued softly. "Remember her teachings." Yes, I would remember that my nanny had taught me many important things— that the worth of my soul was of great value in the eyes of Allah. If I would bring back this soul to him, unspotted by worldly things, then I would indeed have glorified his name. I also knew that if I would ask in faith, believing, I would receive. And so from that day forth, I prayed without ceasing to my Heavenly Father to shorten the days of this war, so that we could return to our homes again.

Chapter Twelve

But it was not yet our time to go home. We had to be patient a little longer. Mams must have struggled, not knowing how her sons and husband were. The last time she had seen her husband, he had been brutally beaten; she wondered if she would ever see him again. She had received no word from the boys in their camps.

The Japanese moved us periodically from camp to camp, perhaps because it would be harder for the men and boys to stay in touch with their wives and loved ones. We were transferred to several camps, mostly around Ambarawah but also as far as Semarang. For this longer journey we traveled in a hot, crowded, and bumpy passenger train whose seats had been removed so we sat on the floor. Every time we moved, the conditions seemed to improve somewhat. In time we were given bunkbeds made of bamboo, which were quite sturdy, although others were even more fortunate and had metal beds to sleep in. We were able to obtain discarded mattresses, and with the mosquito curtains over our heads and our mattresses, we were quite comfortable, although I missed sleeping so close to my mother and being able to feel her warmth during the night.

In some camps we were housed in barracks; in others we lived in vacated European homes. Always we were surrounded by barbed wire and sometimes even bamboo fences. Sometimes we were guarded by very cruel guards, other times by kindly soldiers who left us alone. They must have realized that the chances of a mother and her children trying to escape together were almost impossible; therefore, we enjoyed a greater degree of freedom. As a child, I found it something of an adventure moving to a variety of places; but for my mother, it was undoubtedly very difficult to walk barefoot in the hot sun (as we had no shoes), carrying our meager belongings from camp to camp, and then to reestablish the family again in new surroundings.

The days in the camps were long and dreadful. The women were required to work harder and harder, especially those working in the fields growing food. After working in the fields, we took turns working in the kitchens or the washrooms, which were equally difficult tasks. We were also forced to study Japanese so that we could respond to the Japanese. Their occupation, they assured us, would be a long one, perhaps decades. Everyone in the camp had to register for Japanese lessons; at the same time, all education in the Dutch language was forbidden. The lessons were given in the evening, two or three times a week. Since there were no books available, the lessons were taught by repetition, word for word. Sometimes the instructors droned, sometimes they shouted. Naturally, none of us was really interested in mastering the language of our captors; as long as we could understand the basic commands, we were satisfied.

When "special" visitors came to inspect the camp, the women were forced to clean the premises thoroughly and were often given soap and disinfectant for this purpose. The women did not waste this precious soap on the floors or walls; it was used very, very sparingly so that the rest could be squirreled away for the women to use on their own bodies. Water was also more abundantly available for cleaning purposes, and both children and grownups alike would stand before the walls to be cleaned and refreshed with the precious water before it hit the walls. Everyone took advantage of these visits from special Japanese inspectors to shower and wash clothing, bedding, towels, and anything that needed washing. The downside of these inspections was that often we had to stand outside for hours in the hot sun for endless roll calls while waiting for the visitors to arrive.

Since the Japanese are very clean people, it was mandatory that we sweep not only the barracks, but also the dirt square area where we assembled each time a punishment was to be meted out upon some unfortunate, or when important announcements were made. We made our brooms from palm leaves bound together around a stick, and as it was not tall enough to use by someone standing upright, the worker was forced to bend her body in a most uncomfortable position to be able to sweep.

Everyone was admonished to grow a vegetable patch wherever it was possible to grow anything, because food was becoming scarce and the Japanese almost completely stopped providing us with food. We were fed only once a day—sometimes just a piece of bread or a small portion of rice. We were, however, able to obtain water for the plants that produced our food—mostly vegetables, raised from the seeds we had harvested, and an occasional potato. For the most part we had to fend for ourselves, though it was forbidden to leave the compounds to look for food. Exceptions were made when someone was ill and had to be taken to a hospital in Ambarawah for treatment; only then could we leave the camp.

Most of the barracks had a nurse, usually a Roman Catholic nun, to take care of their immediate needs; often there was a "hospital ward" which had only a few beds. When a child was the patient, the mother or an older sister could usually accompany him, but a guard was always present. Other times a doctor was summoned from either another camp or from outside to treat the patient, and the patient had to stay in the camp. If it was a civilian doctor, we could always count on receiving extra doses of medicine, or a small bottle of oil would change hands, for which we were grateful as we were in dire need of fat in our diet.

When a disease was contagious, the patient was always taken to a hospital outside the camp. If the patient did not survive, the body could be disposed of immediately and buried outside the concentration camp.

In the beginning years of our incarceration, the Japanese would allow people to bury their dead in the little cemetery in Ambarawah, accompanied, of course, by Japanese guards. Sometimes simple coffins of crude lumber were used; but as the war progressed, fewer coffins were made available, and at last the dead were just buried in holes in the ground, and nobody was then allowed to accompany the dead for their burial.

When friends and families were allowed to attend the burials, we were "fortunate" to have been asked to come to the cemetery—at least my mother was, and she would never leave us behind in the camp, and always insisted that we come along. As we walked in the small procession, we would pass fruit stands and food stands along the way. How their aromas would make our mouths water! Of course we were not allowed to purchase anything or stop to take a closer look at those delicacies. However, many times, right under the eyes and noses of the guards, pieces of fruit or food would be offered by natives, which would be hastily hidden in pockets or blouses, to be taken back to camp to share later with loved ones.

During one funeral procession, I could not stop looking at the familiar food stands, and I took frequent deep breaths to savor the aroma that filled the air. The Indonesians at the stands were such beautiful and friendly people, and my heart was heavy because they reminded me of my very own sweet Baboe Kit. How my heart ached for her! Although we were not to speak to the natives, I could not help myself and greeted them in their language as I passed them: "*Selamat pagi*—Good morning!" They returned my greeting softly, almost reverently, so that the guards would not hear: "*Selamat djalan!*—Goodbye, have a nice walk!"

I stopped a moment to take a piece of gravel from my bare foot and lagged behind a little. As I began walking again, a young native girl, younger than I, offered me three pieces of lempur, rolled sticky rice around spiced meat, steamed and wrapped in *dauen pisang,* or banana leaves. I grabbed it quickly and dropped it in the front pocket of my jumper. I could have kissed her but had to be content with a heartfelt thank you: "*Terima kasih banjak!*" As I passed her, I looked back a few times, mouthing my thanks to her but not daring to wave. It was difficult to keep from eating this delicious food that I was carrying, but I had to be patient. I did not want to tell my mother yet about my treasure. This would be my very own secret for a little while and then, oh, what a surprise this was going to be, when I would become a magician and make this delicious treat appear out of my front pocket when we got back in camp! I could not wait to see my mother's surprised face!

It was a beautiful day, and I had learned to enjoy these brief moments of freedom and beauty outside of the camp. I absorbed and enjoyed all the ordinary things free people take for granted until these privileges are taken away from them—fresh air, the smell of shrubs and trees, the scent of fresh-cut grass and flowers. Here I could see for miles without the obstruction of a barbed wire or a bamboo fence, and I took it all in, savoring it, imprinting this bright, happy picture in my memory, to be recalled when life again seemed dark and gray.

At the cemetery, however, I watched a mother say goodbye to her child who had died too early and without need. Had there been no war, this child need not have died and been buried in an unmarked grave. She could have been her mother's companion, perhaps married later and had children of her own, given her mother grandchildren. Now this chance was taken away from her.

Mams kept us at a distance to protect us, but we could hear the mother sobbing and watched her pulled back forcibly from the bier where her child's body lay, before the body was dropped into the hole in the earth.

It was a somber procession that walked back from the cemetery and onto the road leading back to our concentration camp. This mood must have affected the two guards who came with us, because not once did they bark at us to keep us in line. They too were subdued, and even slowed their pace to grant us a moment more of freedom.

On the way to the cemetery, we had passed a small stream with clear water cascading off a large boulder, and the sight of it had made me terribly thirsty. Now, on the way back, it was even more difficult to pass by without being able to drink from it. As always, we were forbidden to speak during our walk, but I was thirsty. I carefully made my way up to the very front of the procession and walked as close as I dared to the Japanese guard. I kept my eyes on him, forcing him to look back to me, and pulled the most pitiful facial expression I could. "I am so very thirsty. Aren't you thirsty, too? Can we *please* take a drink from the water in the stream up ahead?"

Giving no indication that he had even heard me, the guard continued his steady walk forward. Deeply disappointed, I sighed deeply, slowing down my pace and looking longingly to the water, until I had rejoined my mother, Annalise, Wim, and Ellen, who caught up with me.

I had almost resigned myself to wait until our rations were handed out in camp later that day to quench my thirst, when the same guard shouted for us to stop—right in front of the cascading water. What a cruel trick to inflicted upon thirsty prisoners, to let them watch the clear water but not to drink from it. The sun beat down upon us unmercifully, and we were so thirsty. But it was *not* a cruel trick or punishment. "You prisoners, one by one, take a drink from the water, and refresh yourselves. But be quick about it," he shouted.

The procession formed itself quickly in an orderly fashion, one standing behind the other. We drank to our hearts' content, even splashing it into our faces and wetting our bodies where we could. It was heavenly! We stood around smiling, grateful for the refreshment. "Now, you sit down! Rest!" came another shout. We immediately and thankfully complied, soaking our feet in the cool water, although I was careful to guard the front pocket of my jumper to protect my "secret." Mams spoke quietly with the grieving mother, gently splashing water on her head and giving her water from her cupped hands to drink.

When it was time to continue our trek back to the camp, we each took a moment to bow and thank our guards for their generosity and kindness as we filed past them.

That evening, I proudly shared my lempur treat, which we all carefully and slowly enjoyed, savoring each tiny bite. But my surprise was not the only one that evening! Mams also had a surprise. Thanking the Lord for making it possible, she showed us two salted, pickled duck eggs (which must have been at least one hundred years old!!) and an orange. An old Indonesian man had followed us to the cemetery and had handed these to my mother while we were watching the burial. I had not even noticed the old man in the cemetery, although I had been standing right next to my mother at the time.

She then said to us, "Offer unto God thanksgiving; and pay thy vows unto the most High; and call upon me in the day of trouble: I will deliver thee, and thou shalt glorify me." (Ps. 50:14-15.)

Chapter Thirteen

One day, to my surprise, I heard piano music coming from the Japanese barracks. I was drawn to it, and despite my mother's warnings never to go near these barracks, I went. I stood near the door with my body pressed against the bamboo wall and soaked my soul with music—beautiful music.

At last, my curiosity got the better of me and I peeked through the open door to see who was playing this heavenly music. I saw an old piano and a Japanese officer playing it. I stood and listened, forgetting where I was, enthralled by the music. The officer noticed me and motioned for me to come in, but I pulled back. I knew I should leave immediately, but the music held me.

As the officer continued to play, he asked, "Do you like the music?" and I nodded my head.

"Come and listen again," he invited. I was overjoyed, and I did come a few times when I could get away from my mother's all-seeing eyes. I was almost hypnotized by the beauty of the music.

Over time, the officer and I became friendly. "Do you have a family?" I asked. He nodded, and I asked him if he missed them as much as I missed my daddy and my brothers.

"Oh, I miss them very much indeed," he said. "Let me show you my family." He took from his shirt pocket a photograph of a beautiful young Japanese family.

I pointed to a girl in the picture who was about my age. "If you'd like," I said, "I shall be your little girl here in this camp. That way you will not miss your own daughter too much."

One day I was caught talking to the Japanese officer and severely reprimanded by my mother. I told her of the agreement I had made with him, that I was his "adopted daughter." She patted me on the head and told me that I was precocious, an *"enfant terrible."* "When you hear music, you are like a moth that has to go to the light," she said, extracting a promise from me not to talk to him again. "But God and I love you."

I never went back to the barracks to listen to the music from close by. I contented myself with the fragments of the music that floated my way.

Although my mother forbade me to speak with him, she did not tell me that I had to break my agreement to be the officer's little girl, so for the last few months in camp, whenever I would see him, he would wink and I would smile. We had an understanding!

It was this very same officer who came to my mother's barracks and told her that the war would soon be over. "I think we are both so tired of this war," she said. "God be praised. We don't have to be enemies any longer."

He extended his hand to her, and she accepted it.

Once again Mams taught us to "love your enemies, bless them that curse you, do good to them that hate you, and pray for them which despitefully use you, and persecute you; that ye may be the children of your Father which is in heaven." (Matt. 5:44-45.)

Chapter Fourteen

But the final months of the war were slow, and as time ticked away, people were dying of starvation and illness. We were exposed to so much unnecessary cruelty and physical pain. Little children no longer had the strength to cry or to make known their pain or their hunger. Although thousands were interned in this camp, there was an eerie quietness; no one had the strength to speak. At one time people had sung to buoy each other up; now they had stopped singing. There was no small talk, no laughter. The work was performed in silence. The air was filled with hopelessness, and there was no energy left to dream, let alone hope or serve one another. Had the world forgotten us? we wondered. Was there still a God? These were the questions raised in despair.

During a time when some mothers openly stole precious food from their own children to ease their own hunger, how my own mother found the strength and the fortitude to maintain our quality of life during our incarceration is a miracle to me. Mams was sustained by her unfailing and constant faith in Jesus Christ. We witnessed her faith when she offered her prayers, always in thanksgiving first, for what little we had, although sometimes in despair. At times we heard her pray for strength to fight temptations, for the strength to go on: "My God, my God, why hast thou forsaken me? why art thou so far from helping me, and from the words of my roaring?" (Ps. 22:1.) But always, she taught us that "the peace of God, which passeth all understanding, shall keep your hearts and minds through Jesus Christ. . . . Those things, which ye have both learned, and received, and heard, and seen in me, do: and the God of peace shall be with you." (Phil. 4:7, 9.)

The human body needs sugar, fat, calcium, and protein, which we did not get from our captors or received only very sparingly. For protein, Mams taught us to catch grasshoppers or lizards, which were roasted over open fires on a stick. We learned to like these "delicacies," which not only contained protein but also a small amount of fat. Once in a while we were given *gula djawa,* a coarse brown sugar derived from sugar cane, or sugar from a palm, which Mams carefully saved for future use. Before the war, Mother had packed in her black medical bag some coffee candy, or *haagse hopjes,* which she carefully divided among her children. We could not have the whole candy, but had to bite off a piece to make it last longer; then we would suck and suck on it until it was gone.

When we suffered from decayed teeth, it was Annalise who devised a method to take care of us. One night when I kept everyone near us awake with my wailing, Annalise tried to dull the pain by applying clove extract into the cavity. It helped for a while, and I dozed off, but then I would suck on the tooth and the pain would start again. At last she wrapped a sturdy string around the molar and started pulling at it. She had strong fingers and at last the tooth came out. What a relief!

Annalise was often a strength to us in other ways; it was she who could buoy Mams up when she despaired. They both shared the same sense of humor, and I saw them laugh together as well as cry.

To give us strength and hope until deliverance was nigh, Mams told us to watch for a white or pink flower in bloom. This, she said, would be a sign that the war was near an end. "Look for a flowering hibiscus," she whispered to us, holding us tightly; and although there was only a slim chance of ever finding any flower blooming, we watched for it. And so, on very difficult days we would look for our flower, and the search would keep our hope alive.

Chapter Fifteen

We began to hear rumors that the American general, Douglas MacArthur, had returned to the Philippines as he had promised, and that the Japanese there had suffered heavy losses. The Philippines are situated close to Indonesia, so we knew that deliverance was nigh. And yet, still it was such a blissful, unforgettable surprise when the Americans came out of the sky, parachute after parachute. The United States of America had combined forces with troops from New Zealand, Australia, Great Britain, and the Ghurgas from India to liberate us from the Japanese. We knew without doubt that they were American because the paratrooper in the second parachute deployed from the plane had carried a huge American flag, which fluttered in the sky. Although they were only a very small part of these allied forces, they wanted us to know that they were Americans and friendly forces! I shall never forget the Americans in their uniforms and the sight of all their equipment. They were so friendly, so generous, sharing their food and water with us. They were so courageous, and as a girl on the brink of young womanhood, I thought they were terribly handsome, as well. Of course, I fell in love with every one of them. And to this day I am still so very, very grateful for their courage and their sacrifices.

Mams gathered her daughters, small son, and some other children around her and pointed to the sky. "I would like you children to remember always that these young soldiers are coming on the wings of love to bring us freedom. Thank them—and thank God that they came in time," she said to us solemnly.

Allied airplanes flew overhead, dropping pamphlets which read, "Japan has surrendered, the war is over, and you are free!" There were even Dutch planes participating in the fly-over, as we noticed the red, white, and blue colors on their tails. Women and children alike scrambled to grab the pamphlets out of the sky. Our exhilaration knew no bounds. We were free!

During this time, Mams showed us that she was no respecter of persons. She rendered service to friend and foe alike in their hour of need. I witnessed her attending to a Japanese soldier who was shot in the elbow and was in obvious pain. She wrapped his arm and, as he was taken prisoner, offered him a sling made out of the same old sarong shawl that had once covered her beaten, naked body. Within that same hour, I watched as she lovingly rendered service to a dying American soldier by comforting him, cradling his head in her arms, stroking his hair, and reassuring him, time and time again, that his impending death was not in vain—that indeed he had served his God, his fellow men, and his country well.

One young paratrooper landed in a huge banyan tree outside the concentration camp. He was hurt, but he bravely struggled to get untangled from his parachute. Seeing this soldier struggling, Mams asked me to take the black bag and to come along. She took a rifle with a bayonet attached to it from a nearby pile of weapons. We somehow eluded the mines and came to the tree, where, with the help of two others, we were able to take him down.

He was badly wounded. My mother fastened tourniquets above his bleeding knees where his legs had been shot off. A medic ran towards our group and administered morphine to this gravely wounded young man. Then, as his services were needed elsewhere, my mother offered to stay behind and help this soldier.

"Will you pray for me?" the wounded soldier asked, and we knelt beside him. As Mams prayed in English, he began to cry softly. She gently placed his head on her lap, stroking his hair to comfort him. His dogtags read "Smith, F." His religious affiliation was "L.D.S." She did not recognize this designation to be Jewish, Protestant, or Catholic, so she asked him what this "L.D.S." religion was. He replied that it was an American church, founded by an American prophet. He believed that it was the true church of Jesus Christ.

His whole body began to shake, and my mother, thinking that he might go into shock, drew him closer to her to give him some of her body heat. He grew calm and apologized. "I know I'm dying," he said, "and I'm just now realizing that I will never be able to serve a mission for my church." It had always been his dream, he continued, to be able to go on a mission, and he had saved all his earnings while growing up to be able to go. He told us about his mother, who had raised and trained him to fulfill an honorable mission—and now he had to disappoint her.

"You are a righteous, valiant, and honorable missionary of Jesus Christ," my mother comforted him as she cradled his head in her arms. "To me," she said, "you are truly an ambassador of the United States of America and a worthy representative of your American church. You come from a land that represents honor, freedom, and integrity. You must have completed your mission here on earth, and now the Lord is calling you home. Go in peace, my son. Let things go." But he could not let things go yet.

He asked us to look up this L.D.S. church and to learn about it for ourselves. My mother did not know of any L.D.S. churches on the islands in Indonesia, and our chances of ever going to the United States were at that time very slim. But because we knew it would bring peace to his soul, and because he looked at us so pleadingly with his beautiful blue eyes filled with tears, we promised.

While my mother recited the twenty-third psalm in Dutch, Corporal Frank Smith died. He was buried in foreign soil, far from his beloved home in Kansas.

My mother and I walked back to our camp, tired and saddened by this event. We decided to take a different route, walking on a narrow path between ditches through which flowed a mere trickle of water. As we entered the main gate, we saw a bleached pink hibiscus flower blooming next to the ditch. The war was indeed over!

Chapter Sixteen

After the surrender of the Japanese, the allied forces attempted to restore some kind of order. But instead of peace, we soon learned that another war had broken out—a civil war between the native Indonesians, who wanted their independence, and the Dutch. The Indonesians declared their independence from the Dutch on August 17, 1945. We of Dutch/Indonesian descent were caught in the middle, and found that those who had been our friends for a lifetime had now become our enemies because we represented the Dutch authority that governed Indonesia.

The guerrilla fighters, or *peloppers*, as they called themselves, were usually young people eager to gain their independence from the Dutch so they could implement their own state of Indonesia. While the Dutch had been imprisoned by the Japanese, these Indonesians, under the leadership of Sukarno, had begun to persuade the native Indonesians to fight for their independence and succeeded far better than they had hoped. Discarded weapons and vehicles from the Japanese were confiscated, and guerrilla warfare launched against the Dutch government, the Dutch people, and the Dutch Indonesians. In fact, war was declared on anybody who was pro-Dutch! Although now free, we faced more bloodshed. Although free, we had no home to return to; the *pro tem*, or interim, Indonesian government had confiscated all our properties. This period is known as the *Bersiap* time, a time of great sorrow, of deep mourning for the Dutch/Indonesian people, who though technically "free," were without homes, without clothing, without food.

Thus we became refugees and were evacuated to another camp for shelter and protection. The International Red Cross provided for our needs, for food, clothing, and housing. Our first "home" after the war was an old fort in Ambarawah, Fort Williams, built in 1848 by the Dutch. The cells were covered with bars, and the cell doors were very thick and heavy. It was a frightening place to be. We slept on mattresses on the cement floor and received food once a day. However, the food supply was limited and hampered by the *peloppers,* "extremists" as we called them, who were determined to keep the Dutch on their knees. Placed in this fort for our protection, it was now the Japanese—our former enemies—who protected us from the uprising Indonesians until the Japanese were replaced by the Ghurgas from India.

Posted in front of our cell, for our protection, stood a Ghurgan soldier, who stood guard with his machine gun and knitted a sweater to pass the time and calm his nerves, he told us with a smile.

In this new place Mams allowed us more freedom to explore, and we roamed the corridors, now conversing casually with our protectors, some of whom had once been our enemies. One day, Annalise, Ellen, Wim, and I left our mother behind in our cell, which we shared with another family of five, to walk from the lower level to our upper level quarters. Suddenly we heard an enormous commotion. Our sharp-eyed Japanese protectors had noticed some bushes and small trees moving around outside the camp in the wide-open field. "Identify yourselves," they had shouted, and the bushes and trees opened fire upon our camp. Immediately our defenders returned fire.

The Ghurgas and Japanese had set up automatic weapons along the corridor for our defense, but to return to the safety of our cell, we had to go through these corridors! We ran as fast as we could, Annalise behind us pulling Wim, whose little legs could not carry him as fast as his older sisters' legs could go.

At last we reached the upper level and our cell door. Our Ghurgan soldier friend, standing at his post front of our cell, opened the massive cell door to let us in. As he was closing the door behind Annalise, a grenade exploded where he stood. Mams pulled us immediately under a mattress for protection. While the massive cell door protected us against the explosion, our compassionate Ghurgan friend was killed immediately. We found part of his unfinished sweater at the far end of the corridor.

The situation became increasingly dangerous, and it was decided to move us to another camp. The extremists were gaining ground and had taken over the whole area. They were very dangerous and had murdered many of the Dutch women and children as they were on their way back to their homes, or what was left of them after the Japanese occupation. The women and children had returned to their homes hoping to find their liberated husbands and fathers. Instead, they encountered this onslaught. The revolutionaries had also ransacked and plundered many of the Dutch-Indonesian homes and terrorized their owners, searching for money and valuables to support their cause. It was a time of horrors, because most civilians were powerless to do anything. To what authority could they go to complain or to find protection from these revolutionaries? Consequently, many Indos fled from their homes and found themselves in these "protective camps" along with those of us coming from the Japanese camps. Many were as destitute as those of us who had come out of the Japanese camps. Others had been able to take a few more belongings with them when they fled their homes, but also had difficulties carrying all their possessions when moving from camp to camp for their protection. Our meager possessions were still securely packed in the large leather suitcase with our family name painted on it in bold letters with white paint.

We were taken by open truck from Ambarawah to Camp Halmahera in the city of Semarang, which previously had housed the women and children under Japanese occupation. We avoided the main roads, traveling on a side road where we would be less likely to encounter the extremists. Because of the danger of the roads, the convoy of trucks was driven and protected by English soldiers who carried machine guns.

The sky was overcast and threatened to rain any moment, so the drivers decided to stop to put the covers on the truck when we reached the outskirts of the town. It appeared to be a relatively safe spot to stop, as the road was surrounded by lush bushes and tall trees, and looked very idyllic and tranquil. Because of the number of trucks in our convoy, it took some time before all the trucks had been covered and the drivers had agreed upon what direction and how far to take this road.

Many of the women took this opportunity to let the little

children relieve themselves beside the road. Ellen always seemed to have the need to use the bathroom, usually at inconvenient or at inappropriate times, but especially when she was under stress. We were admonished to be as quiet as possible and to get back into the trucks as quickly as possible. I followed as Mams led Ellen toward a little stream that flowed alongside the road, where we would wash ourselves.

Without warning, we heard shooting from a distance on the other side of the road, so we ran back to the truck for protection.

"Crawl beneath the trucks, over here, where it's safe," shouted the British soldiers who had begun returning the fire.

As we ran toward the trucks, one of my shoes became stuck in the mud. This was my very first pair of good shoes, and they were my priceless possession. I had received them from the Red Cross after the war, and I intended to keep them. I stopped to pull my shoe from the mud, and in that way became separated from my mother.

I quickly crawled under the nearest truck and covered my ears with both hands to dull the sound of the shooting, pulled my legs under my body, and curled into a ball, making myself as little as possible. My mother and Ellen were on the other side, behind the second truck. I could not see Annalise and Wim, and I felt isolated and alone, so I did the only thing I could do—I prayed through my tears.

The band of guerrilla troops came closer and closer and the shooting became more intense, some bullets whizzing close by me and hitting the truck I was under. I knew some people were struck by bullets, because I could hear their cries. I wished I could be closer to my mother, and I looked around. She must have been wishing the same thing, because she looked over to where I was and smiled encouragingly. I started to move in her direction, but she signaled for me to stay where I was.

"Put down your weapons and surrender," a loud voice ordered from the bushes behind us. The words were in Bahasa Indonesia, now the official language of the country. "You are surrounded."

The shooting stopped and the peloppers came out of the bushes on both sides of the road. "*Merdeka, merdeka, merdeka!*" they shouted, which meant "Freedom!" or "Independence!" The British officer in charge gave the command to our soldiers to put their weapons down, then he wrapped his white handkerchief on the end of his rifle and held it high above his head.

During this brief pause in the shooting, I gathered myself up and dashed to my mother's side. She immediately put her arms around me and held me close, but her eyes remained fixed to the place where the loud voices were coming from. She listened intently as orders were given to the British soldiers.

I was surprised to see how young the peloppers were, some no older than fourteen or fifteen. Their weapons were merely long bamboo rods with razor-sharp tips at the ends, which they used to terrorize people. Some were perhaps in their mid- or late twenties, and carried guns confiscated from the Japanese. There were only about twenty of them, and if they had not had their weapons, we could have overpowered them. It was only by chance that they had come upon us, and now their leader would no doubt use this opportunity to prove that he was a patriot.

The peloppers stood with their weapons drawn and pointed at us, ready to shoot at any time, as the leader commanded us to come out from under the trucks. "Stand against the sides of the trucks with your hands up in the air," he shouted. The few people who had been hurt could sit, but still they were required to raise their hands in the air. Annalise took this opportunity to run with Wim to where we were standing.

The leader strutted back and forth, smiling, proud as a peacock at this conquest. As he moved closer to where we were standing, my mother fixed her eyes on him and cocked her head, listening intently, as if trying to remember something. Suddenly she smiled, and I could tell that she had remembered what she was trying to think of.

She let go of our hands (which she was holding, contrary to the order to keep her hands up high), stepped forward, and walked towards the leader, stopping directly in front of him. Then she spoke softly but tersely to him in the local dialect.

"Si Sudarman, Si Sudarman, did I save your life for you to become a rabble-rouser? What are you doing to us? How dare you frighten little children and wound innocent people? Have we not suffered enough under the Japanese? I thought you were our friend!!"

The leader looked surprised at this lecture, and then ashamed. He was indeed Si Sudarman, our former *kebun*, or gardener, whom my mother had nursed back to health after his legs had been crushed by a falling tree during a thunderstorm.

Si Sudarman bowed deeply before her, apologizing profusely for not recognizing her right away. The war had changed her appearance, but her voice was still the same. "*Ibu,* I am glad to see you, glad you are alive after the Japanese occupation," he said. Yes, of course, he was still her friend and he would remain her eternal, ever-remembered friend. He would consider it a great honor if she would still be his friend as well. How could he make restitution for his unrighteous acts? he asked.

Si Sudarman took the time to greet us children, too, in a most respectful manner. "I am so ashamed for the hurt I have caused you," he repeated over and over. "*Ampun, memaafkan.* Please forgive me."

My mother had addressed him in the local dialect, which was not understood by most present, and he was thus able to save face when she scolded him. He could still be the patriot that he wanted to be, and now had become an even better one—a patriot with compassion, not one filled with hate or given to cruelty. His country and his countrymen would be proud of him. We could tell that he was grateful and relieved. Like his fellow Javanese, Si Sudarman was a tenderhearted, refined, and cultured man, a man of integrity who was torn between loyalties to his Indo friends and to his country.

Si Sudarman ordered his men to put their weapons away, then told all of us that we could relax and care for the wounded. He asked my mother to serve as an interpreter to converse with the English military escort. A survey of the damage done to the trucks revealed that only one had been demobilized. This meant that some of the luggage had to be left behind if all the people were to find places in the other trucks. Everybody cooperated; little children were held on laps, even by strangers, and some people were sitting on their bags to make room for one another's belongings.

We had already left most of our worldly necessities behind. Still, when one Indo-Chinese woman had to leave her rolled-up mattress behind, she began to cry and wring her hands. Then we learned that she had sewn her family's valuables into the cotton of the mattress, and this was the real reason for her emotional outburst.

She was able to negotiate with the peloppers, who allowed her to cut open the mattress—for a ridiculously high price, of course. She took the leftover items and money out, wrapped it all in a sarong, then climbed back into the truck, all the while grumbling and moping that this was highway robbery. We had to laugh about this. Of course it was highway robbery—we were in the middle of one!

Si Sudarman took six of his older peloppers to ride "shotgun" on the trucks, and soon we were on our way to our next "protection camp." Ironically, we were more shielded than we had been previously because of the red and white merdeka flags that were placed on each truck. We encountered two roadblocks on the main road we took, but Si Sudarman was able to convince the guerrillas to let us through unharmed.

Once in friendly territory, the English took over again and we said goodbye to our "enemies." Mams took Si Sudarman's hand in both of hers. "In behalf of all these people here, may I express our sincere thanks and gratitude for your compassion and mercy shown towards us," she said. "You can be sure that these acts have been recorded in heaven and were pleasing to Allah." All the others joined in, and good wishes were exchanged. "*Sampai jumpa,* until we meet again" and "*Selamat jalan,* have a good trip!" As our trucks rumbled on, we waved at this little group of men until we could not see them anymore.

Chapter Seventeen

Our camp in Semarang consisted of several European homes on Djalan Halmahera. We lived in No. 35. The kitchen was situated in the middle of this camp along with the latrines. Nearby stood a small hospital and dispensary that used to be a Roman Catholic convent. Barbed wire and a huge bamboo wall still surrounded the whole compound.

At the crossroads of two streets on a large square stood several trees. One of them we nicknamed the "gumball tree," because its fruits reminded us candy-starved children of gumballs!

In these camps we had the freedom to come and go as we pleased, but it was not always safe to do so. Although the city itself was less affected by the changes in the country than the nearby little villages, it was not wise to be out past dark. In fact, a curfew was put in place for our protection.

Food was more readily available as we received more and more provisions, so little by little we regained our strength. Every once in a while we received Red Cross or Care packages from the U.S. or Canada that contained clothing, vitamins, corned beef, powdered milk and eggs, and even American cigarettes, which my mother bartered for vegetables and rice. Of course, our favorite items from the packages were the delicious Hershey candy bars!

My mother still had some money left over from what she had brought with her into our concentration camp, which she had hidden in the bottom of our black bag. Fortunately, the Japanese, who were constantly looking for money among the prisoners and would often search us, never thought to look or asked to look into my mother's black bag. With this money and the small allowance given to each person, she was able to find better food for us than that given to us in the camp.

However, life was still painfully uncertain. We had not heard from the boys or my father. Now the task was at hand to find out which members of our family had survived this ordeal. My mother walked from one Red Cross post to another, making inquiries about our family. To her sorrow, she learned that Herbie had died and Daniel was seriously ill with cholera. But she was overjoyed to learn that he was in a Catholic hospital right there in Semarang.

My father had left word through the Red Cross that he had been transported from his latest camp in Balikpapan on Borneo via Tandjong Priok in West Java, near Djarkarta, on to Soesterberg, in Holland, to receive much-needed medical aid. The Red Cross workers assured my mother that my father would be contacted in Holland and informed of our location so that he could contact us.

Mams learned from the survivors who had worked on the railroads in Burma that her brother, Herbert, had succumbed to starvation. Her half-brother, James, was safe in Bandoeng, and her youngest brother, John, who had been trained as a pilot in Arizona and had participated in the liberation from the Japanese, was now in Australia, recuperating from a shattered elbow. From the Red Cross she received addresses where she could contact her brothers. To be on the safe side, she also gave the Red Cross information as to how others could get in touch with her.

Mams mourned Herbie's death deeply. She became very quiet and pensive, but nevertheless found comfort as she surrendered herself to the faith and knowledge of the love of Christ. She knew her son, mercifully released from his suffering and pain, was now out of his misery. He was now safe in heaven, surrounded by God's love. But oh, how she wished she could have seen him one last time before his death! Still, she was grateful for the few years she had had to love and nurture him, and to enjoy his spirit. Herbie had been called to his heavenly home, and she had to let him go. Other things now demanded her attention.

For example, she had two other sons to think about. Daniel was in the hospital, alive but seriously ill. And upon receiving word that Konrad was on his way to join us, she knelt and offered a prayer of thanksgiving. For the lives of these two sons she was grateful. Yes,

God had been good to her and she would overcome her grief; she *had to* overcome it for her other children's sakes. Her family was not yet out of danger; she needed to find a home for them and she had so much to arrange. But with God's help she could do anything; and so, once again, my mother relied on the goodness and mercy of God.

My oldest brother, Konrad, had been interned in the boys' camp in Ambarawah, not far from where we were first interned. He hitchhiked and walked all the way to find us in Halmahera. His curly hair was unkempt, he had outgrown his clothes, which were now tattered and stained, and his eyeglasses had been broken and taped.

He was covered with lice and had a festering, open wound on his leg, so Mams took him directly to the dispensary and attended to his wound. Then he was allowed to take a shower, and his head was shaved to get rid of the lice. (In fact, all our hair had been cut short to get rid of our own head lice—a souvenir from being in a concentration camp.) Konrad also had trouble expressing himself and stuttered, a scar from the war that took him years to overcome. His face, once cheerful and vibrant, was now somber, and his eyes were downcast. How I missed the sound of his laughter!

While we waited for Daniel to get well, Mams visited him every day. Konrad accompanied her on the strenuous trek to the hospital, while Annalise stayed with us. At the hospital where Daniel was staying, Mams was pleased to find the very same nurse who had worked in the hospital where she had given birth to her children. Like Mams, Sister Renata had survived a concentration camp and was able to tell her of mutual friends in the camp. Sister Renata took it upon herself to look after Daniel, which was a great comfort to my mother.

Finally the day came when we were able to bring Daniel home from the hospital. He looked so terribly thin and his skin was still yellow from jaundice. As he was too weak to walk all the way to camp Halmahera, Mams hired a *betjak*—a three-wheeled bicycle, pedaled by manpower, a popular mode of transportation in Asia.

On the way home, Mams treated each of us to a delicious fruit popsicle, which we bought from a vendor on the street, to celebrate our family reunion. Since Ellen and I could not choose between so many flavors, we each chose a different fruit flavor and split it. That way we would each have two different fruit flavors!

That evening we held our first family devotional as a complete family, just like the old times. We missed Herbie and our father, but were comforted to know that both were being cared for. It was such a heavenly feeling to be together again; everyone in our immediate family was now accounted for. I could see that Mams, like a devoted mother hen, was grateful to have her little chicks back under her protective wings again. Herbie, she knew, was with God. For the first time in many, many months, Mams slept peacefully that night.

Chapter Eighteen

The next morning we could hear our mother humming happily as she went about her household chores. It felt so good to see her renewed energy and feel that she was at peace.

The rainy season was at hand, and we had no warm clothing to shield us from the chill. Mams had discovered a huge pool table covered with green felt, so she carefully cut the felt with a sharp razor blade and sewed together three little green jackets for Wim, Ellen, and myself. The three of us became known as "the three little green peas in a pod," but we didn't care; we were proud of our warm jackets!

The house also held a reproduction of a painting of a cute, smiling Dutch boy with blue eyes and blonde hair. Immediately smitten by that cute face, I asked my mother if I could take this picture with me. My mother consented, but I would have to take care of it myself. I also confiscated a worn-out storybook with pictures, which I devoured immediately.

Mams decided that we should join my father as soon as possible and requested evacuation to Holland. This would take time, we knew. When the Dutch soldiers took over Kamp Halmahua, we were notified that we were to move to yet another camp, which would serve as a "collection point" for transportation to West Java. From there we would eventually be evacuated to Holland by boat.

Annalise was ecstatic when she learned that we would be staying at the very same high school that she and Konrad had attended before the war had broken out. She immediately took us on a tour through the school.

It was a huge school, with an auditorium, a swimming pool, and a gym as well as a track and field area with tennis courts, soccer and hockey fields, and *korfbal* courts. *Korfbal* is a form of basketball, except it has three courts, and the game is played co-ed with twelve people on each team, two boys and two girls in each court, trying to get the ball into a *korf,* which is an actual basket without a bottom, attached to a pole without the benefit of a backboard. It is a popular game next to soccer. Because of the lack of equipment, the kids improvised and played soccer with an empty can and hockey with sticks made out of tree limbs.

The classrooms were converted into dormitories with bunkbeds. For the first time in almost four years we slept in beds with real sheets, a pillow, and a thin blanket. It felt so good, so rich, and so clean! Our clothes, too, smelled delightfully clean from the laundry soap we had received to wash them with. No longer did we have to stand in line to use the bathrooms. There were plenty of showers and bathrooms, and fewer people who wanted to use them at the same time.

It was in this camp that we started to live "normally" again. We could walk around where we wanted (in shoes to protect our feet from the heat), eat as much as we wanted, and drink as much as we wanted. We had access to medical attention if we needed it. It felt good to be *free* again—to hear birds chirping, see the colorful butterflies flying around us, and even smell the flowers that were growing there. We had green grass around us—no more dry, dusty dirt to walk in. No one ordered us around anymore. There was no more screaming, no more fighting, no more bickering, and no more noise from machine guns.

It was here that we went to formal church services for the first time since our captivity. It was an emotional sensation when, as a congregation, we sang hymns of thanksgiving and praise to God. As we took communion, many tears were shed remembering those who had lost their lives.

"We are involved in yet another war," the clergyman reminded us. "Many more among us here today might still lose their lives. Please be prudent but be brave," he said, then blessed the congregation. We ended the services by singing the Dutch national anthem, *Wilhelmus van Nassauen,* and departed with renewed faith, hope, and courage to face the future.

Here I saw my very first movie pictures, which were shown every

Saturday afternoon in the big auditorium. They were mostly American movies, in which the Americans were portrayed as very happy-go-lucky people who were very loud and laughed a lot. They had all the comforts of life and lived lavishly in big homes, but I was surprised to see that they had no servants. The American countryside was so beautiful with its purple mountains, yellow deserts, green pastures, and blonde beaches. The sun seemed to shine there all the time. Never did I see a movie that depicted the dreary winter. It was all very fascinating, and I decided that one day I would visit that beautiful country.

We learned a few American songs such as "Sentimental Journey" and "Don't Fence Me In." My favorite was "You Are My Sunshine," which we would sing over and over again. Mams would never restrain us from singing; rather, she encouraged us to sing. It must have done her heart good to hear her children sing and be happy again.

Because there were more Indo children there, we felt more at ease and would join them more readily in their children's games such as "Here I Throw Down My Handkerchief" or "Pin the Tail on the Donkey." Life in this particular camp was a very happy experience.

Meanwhile, the British troops were replaced by Dutch marines and other soldiers who had come from Holland to fight the war, and our own KNIL soldiers (Royal Dutch Indonesian Army) joined them as well. Our peace here was interrupted when the guerrillas came closer to the city. Heavy fighting was reported on the other side of the city, with many casualties. The evacuation effort intensified, and we were taken by truck to the Semarang Airport to catch a plane to Batavia. There we found that the guerrillas had surrounded the airport.

Our plane was parked on the tarmac, which was a distance from the hangar where we were dropped off. We placed our luggage in a heap on the outside of the building and hurriedly sought cover from the shooting. The KNIL soldiers suggested that those who could run fast should take their luggage and run it over to where the plane was parked, then board the plane as fast as they could.

Konrad and Daniel were ready to go, but Mams would not let them. Instead, she called us over to have a little prayer. "You are *not* going over there and expose yourselves to gunshots," she insisted. "If we miss this plane, we miss it. There will be other aircraft. I will not risk losing any of you here. That is that!"

The younger people who dashed out made it safely into the plane, but many were forced to leave their belongings behind. Predictably, our family missed this airplane. But Mams refused to leave the airport. She would wait until another plane arrived.

The peloppers were too impatient to wait for another aircraft to land so they could capture it. Or perhaps they lost courage when they learned that it was no easy thing to take over an airport, especially when they had to contend with the KNIL military people. So they withdrew from the airport.

After a four-hour wait, another airplane managed to land. After it had refueled, it would take us to Batavia. As always, our mother had been right to wait. Now we could enjoy our very first airplane flight!

Most important, we still had our one suitcase, which was identified with our family name in huge white painted letters. As it was loaded on the plane, one of the soldiers held up a sewing machine and asked my mother, "Is this sewing machine yours?" We could see that the name on it was the same as ours, but it wasn't our sewing machine.

"No," my mother said, "I am not so lucky to have a sewing machine."

"Well," he shouted, "it has your name on it, and no one else in this company has the same name as yours. You had better take it!" And with that, he heaved the sewing machine into the plane. Konrad placed it in front of my seat next to him so I could use it as a footstool and put my feet on it for safekeeping.

As soon as the propellers from the aircraft started to turn and the plane began to taxi, a queasy feeling entered my stomach. When mother saw me turn green, she left her seat to ask the airman standing near the back door of the plane for a bag and a glass of water. Although Konrad tried to divert my attention from my airsickness by pointing out the small houses and cars beneath the plane, looking out of the window made me even more sick. Fortunately, Mams brought the bag in time, but unfortunately, my poor rag doll Pop Mientje was a hapless victim of my vicious retching. Finally, the airman gave me a spoonful of a white powder to take with a few sips of water, and I was able to sleep for the rest of the trip.

That evening we landed safely in Batavia, but Konrad had to carry me out of the plane, as I did not awaken until we had arrived in a holding area where we were given temporary shelter. I was so relieved to be on solid ground again!

Chapter Nineteen

In Batavia, now called Djakarta, the capitol of Indonesia, the streets were crowded with bicycles, *betjaks, dokars* (horse drawn carriages), buses, motorbikes, and even a few cars—all the people going in every direction, although the traffic flow was effectively controlled with the traffic lights or uniformed policemen. There was noise everywhere, but it was not the noise of war we had been used to, although the streets were filled with men in Dutch, KNIL, and British uniforms.

We children found this a very confusing but fascinating place to be. We were directed to an area in Batavia where other evacuated people had also gathered to be shipped to Holland. We were given a garage for housing while we waited. There was just enough space for all seven of us to sleep on the floor on the thin mattresses that were provided for us.

My mother used her ingenuity to divide our quarters into "boys" and "girls" rooms by draping down a discarded parachute from a piece of wire. This gave us girls some privacy when we were dressing. Our bathroom facilities were outside in the back of the main house, and had formerly been used by the servants of the people who used to live in the main house. The bathroom consisted of a closed-in toilet and a barrel of water, collected from rainwater, from which we could scoop out water out to bathe ourselves. At least there was privacy, although we still had to share these facilities with several other families. Nevertheless, we were much more comfortable than we had been in the camps, and for that we were grateful.

Since there were no kitchen privileges to speak of, Mams fixed our food on charcoal fires outside. Again, while this was not the comfort she had been used to before the war, it was better than in the camps where she had to use firewood to stoke the fires. For food we received ration coupons to shop at a military commissary, along with a small allowance that my mother used to buy fresh vegetables and sometimes fruit from the local open marketplace.

We found the people in Batavia friendly, which reminded us that the older people did not have animosity towards us; it was the younger generation who wanted the Dutch and pro-Dutch out of their country. It was such a joy to mingle with the people again, to be able to buy and relish native tidbits and refreshments from the little food stands. We cherished this new freedom.

Our diet was rice, three times a day, which was a treat after the lack of food in the camps. For protein we received canned corned beef, and my mother was very innovative in fixing various tasty dishes with this corned beef. Often she bartered it for fish, spices, or other products. The "black market" flourished, and one could buy anything—for a price.

Our house was behind the military housing, and my mother frequently invited the soldiers to stay for dinner when they came to visit us. They were starved for family companionship, and of course my mother was willing to provide that for them. In return they brought us fruit and other provisions that we lacked, such as washing soap or bleach.

On those occasions, we would all sit outside on mats or old folding chairs until late in the evening. Because of the curfew, there was nowhere to go and we were happy to sit with the soldiers and talk in the dark, as it grew dark very early and the lights could not be lit after a certain hour. So we sat outside in the dark and reminisced about the "good old times" in Indonesia as well as Holland, or shared war experiences, or discussed the present political situation. When a Dutch or Indo soldier had a guitar, we sang folks songs together.

My mother often invited the soldiers to participate in our evening devotionals, which they eagerly accepted. Many were happy for the opportunity to pray to our Heavenly Father, to give thanks and to ask for protection.

During the day, usually after she had been to the market, my mother sewed dresses and rompers for the girls, using her new sewing machine and material bartered for discarded parachutes from the

Allied military. The two older boys received khaki shirts and trousers.

During our stay in Batavia, we received thorough medical attention as part of our preparation for evacuation to Holland. We were given a special soap to get rid of our head lice and had our hair neatly and stylishly cut. Medication was prescribed to get rid of our tapeworms, and Konrad received special medicine for his open sores. Our teeth were checked and filled or pulled if necessary. We began to feel like civilized human beings again.

In March of 1946, my mother received notice that we were to report to the administrative offices to obtain our passes for the long-awaited evacuation to Holland. We would travel on the troop transport ship *Kota Agung,* which would leave from Tjandung Priok and sail to Amsterdam, Holland! How we looked forward to our reunion with our father!

I was excited, too, to see Holland, although I had no idea what it would be like. I envisioned that it would be a friendly place, a wonderful place, although the Dutch soldiers told us that the weather could be cold and damp, unlike the Dutch Indies.

Leaving her homeland must have been a difficult time for my mother. This was the land of her birth. She had been raised and educated here, and she loved this beautiful country with its cobalt blue sky, the green variegated terraced rice paddies with the gray water buffaloes pulling the ploughs in the fields, the swaying palm trees, the majestic waringin trees, the abundance of colorful fragrant flowers and fauna of this land. Here the thundering waterfalls cascaded down into powerful wide rivers flowing slowly through the countryside, and the sun came up quickly in the mornings and set amidst gorgeous colors in the evening. Here the smell of charcoal fires mingled with the familiar odors of food prepared with an immense variety of spices, for which this land was famous.

In this land the people lived close to their mother earth, taking from her only what they needed, and thereby guarding her fertility, her ability to provide for future generations. The people lived simply, content with small pleasures, obedient and faithful to those in authority over them and especially to their gods, whether they were Hindu, Muslim, or Christian.

It must have been heartbreaking for my mother to leave her home in the Dutch East Indies. But she hid her pain on the day that the seven of us climbed aboard the troop transport ship *Kota Agung*, our belongings packed away in only two suitcases. She would never complain, never express her longing for the warmer climate when she was cold and shivering in our apartment in Holland, trying to conserve the coals which were then rationed. She never complained of homesickness or her longing for the native Indonesian food, which she could not prepare in Holland because of lack of the necessary spices or vegetables.

My sweet mother girded up her loins and took fresh courage as she led us to our new land.

Chapter Twenty

Our family was one of the first to be evacuated to Holland from the Dutch East Indies in a converted freighter. The Dutch soldiers had used these ships to get to Indonesia to fight the civil war, and these ships returned to Holland with the sick and the refugees. The other refugees who followed us were transported in gigantic cruise ships such as the *SS Orange* and the *SS Johan Van OldeBarneveldt.*

Our ship was smaller but very comfortable as we traveled through the Strait of Malacca, across the Indian Ocean into the Red Sea, and through the Suez Canal. Because I suffered from seasickness, I spent most of the thirty or so days on board ship in the sick bay, where I was well cared for by the military personnel.

From my first day on board, my travel sickness prevented me from taking food or water, which I could not keep in my stomach. Consequently, I became dehydrated and developed a high fever. My mother tried to nurse me herself and attempted to persuade me to eat by bringing the most delicious food to my bunk from the mess hall. She even brought me a shiny red apple, something I had not seen for nearly four years—since before the war! And yet, even that could not persuade me to take a bite. Just the faintest smell of food turned my stomach.

And so I was taken to the sick bay for the duration of the trip. The only time I was able to come on deck was when our ship went through the Suez Canal, where it glided smoothly through the canal. My brother Konrad carried me to the main upper deck, where I was placed on a deck chair. I breathed in the sweet smell of outside air and stared wide-eyed at the sphinx and the magnificent pyramids of Egypt as we by passed them in our ship. I have never forgotten the gleaming white sand of the desert or the sparkling blue sky overhead, with the sphinx and pyramids silhouetted against it, or the sight of the line of merchants who passed these ancient monuments with camels heavy laden with bulky merchandise, wrapped in colorful blankets. *I have left the ugliness behind me,* I thought to myself. *The world is beautiful after all.*

This picturesque landscape meant even more to us when our mother reminded us that this was the same land of Egypt where the prophet Moses had brought the Hebrew people out of captivity. Under the guiding hand of the Lord, Moses had parted the Red Sea so that the children of Israel could go safely on their way to the promised land. Similarly, our ship, the *Kota Agung,* had just left the Red Sea and was now taking our family to *our* "promised land"!

At Port Said, Egypt, the International Red Cross had set up a reception center for us. When the ship docked, we were deluged with merchants who had come on board to sell leather goods. They parked their little boats against our ship and bargained with us, standing in their unsteady little boats, trying to sell us wallets, handbags, footstools, shoes, jewelry, and hats. I was fascinated at the exchange of goods for money. The money was thrown down or lowered down in a handkerchief, and the merchandise was thrown up or put in a basket to be hauled up by the buyer, the whole exchange accompanied by loud voices and the waving of hands. To celebrate this special occasion, Mams bought each of the girls a little purse; the boys received leather wallets. We children convinced her to buy something for herself as well, so she bought a leather handbag. We called her bag the "Attica handbag," in honor of the Egyptian harbor of the same name. She kept that bag for years, and whenever she needed it, she would say, "Children, hand me my Attica."

From the ship we were transported by rail to the Red Cross reception center, where we would receive winter clothing and shoes to wear in the cold Dutch weather. Our next stop was Port Said, where we were warmly welcomed by the Red Cross. There, we were saddened and frightened by the sight of so many beggars along the street, many very aggressive and bold as they waved their crippled arms or legs in front of us or tugged on our arms. But we had nothing to give them!

We were ushered into a huge hangar-type building, which was

decorated with the flags of many nations hanging from the ceiling on long strings. Long tables and chairs had been set up for us to sit on, and we were served tea and cakes, as well as fruit and meat pies. There were also candies, chocolates, and cookies in abundance. We could eat as much as our hearts desired! And when we were done the workers packed dozens of goodies in little boxes for us to take with us.

Now that I was on solid ground and no longer felt seasick, I wanted to eat everything in sight, but my stomach would not let me. So I nibbled at a few treats, then reluctantly packed the rest in my box, looking forward to the time I would be able to eat these goodies later on.

We were next taken to another hangar that looked like a huge clothing store. There we were fitted with winter clothes from socks and underwear to sweaters, skirts and dresses to coats and fur hats. The best part of it all was that everything fit perfectly! How pleased I was to have beautiful, dainty, and lady-like new shoes!

In addition to our new clothes, we each received a new suitcase to carry all our new belongings—clothing, handkerchiefs, lotion, face cream, hair brushes and combs, toothbrushes, nail scissors, even sewing kits. All the necessities that one usually takes for granted, but that we had lived without so many years during our confinement. We had to be shown how to use the special Pond's face cream we were given for our sunburnt faces. Sixteen-year-old Annalise even received nail polish!

How grateful we were for all the things given to us, and how happy I was to be able to leave the ship at last and to gain some relief from the constant seasickness! But too soon it was time to reboard our ship and begin the last leg of our journey home.

Laden with our packages, suitcases, and bundles, we boarded the train to take us to the harbor. When we got off the train, the beggars were still there. Some touched us with their fingers or stroked us pleadingly with their hands. We did not speak their language, but we understood only too well what they were saying. They were hungry, they did not have a job, and most likely they did not have a place to live. My heart bled for them. I knew what it was like.

Impulsively, I handed my box of goodies to an emaciated woman with two little children at her side and one in her arms. She grabbed the box from my hand and almost ran with it to the far corner of the platform, where she ripped open the box and divided the pieces of pie and cookies among her children.

When we boarded the ship, we discovered that all my mother's children had given away their boxes of goodies.

We knew how they felt, these beggars with nothing, and we had received so much this day. We were returning to a ship where we could take a warm shower to wash off the dust, where we would be fed delicious and nutritious meals, where we could drink anytime we were thirsty, where we would have a clean, comfortable bed to sleep in, and where we would be safe. How grateful we were that our lot had changed, and we were reminded that the Lord had been watching over us. He had been merciful to us, He had protected us, and He was now leading us to a new land.

Going through the Mediterranean Sea was not as rough as I had anticipated, and I was able to get out of sick bay more often to enjoy the sunshine on deck, but I could not stay up there for long periods of time. At the slightest rocking movement of the ship I was overcome with nausea again.

During peaceful moments, the dolphins played around the ship, and huge albatross birds flew over us and followed the ship before hurtling themselves into the water in search of fish.

The day we passed the Rock of Gibraltar as we turned north into the Atlantic Ocean was beautiful and calm, and the weather was mild as the ship passed the peninsula of Spain and Portugal. But as we proceeded further north the weather suddenly changed, and we found ourselves in a furious storm that rocked the freighter back and forth. I found myself back in the sick bay, where I was so ill that I lost track of time and place. All I wanted to do was sleep. . . .

Chapter Twenty-One

"Wake up," said a pleasant voice. It was one of the nurses. "Wouldn't you like to take a shower? We are approaching the Dutch coast, and it is a beautiful day. The ocean has calmed and the sun is shining. It is time to clean up and get ready. I want you to eat something. How does a soft-boiled egg and toast sound?"

It did not sound good at all to me, but I felt much better after I had showered and dressed in my own clothes instead of the hospital gown I had worn for so long.

The nurse returned with a tray full of food. There was toast and marmalade, eggs, fruit, juices, milk, tea, and crackers. I carefully ate the egg and toast, and they stayed down!

The doctor was pleased to see that I could eat. "You are doing very well," he said. "I am very proud of you that you are eating. Will you eat some oatmeal for me? How about another egg?"

Yes, I thought I could eat another, I said.

"I want you to promise me that you will eat at least three times a day from now on. We want you to regain your strength," he said as he squeezed my thin arm. After he gave me a final injection, he gave his permission for me to leave with Mams, who had brought me some warm clothing to wear. I grabbed my rag doll and was ready to go. I could not wait to leave the ship!

It was Konrad who again carried me upstairs to the upper deck, where Annalise had procured a deck chair and blanket for me. Together we joined the people at the ship's railing who watched anxiously for the first sign of the Dutch coast. This was a momentous occasion.

One of the ship's crew members approached my mother and

directed us to a landing which stood higher than the deck, from which we had an excellent view and could see out over the throng of gathered people. What a treat!

Because the land in Holland lies below sea level, the ship had to be docked first, transferring from one sluice to another, before going through the *Noordzee kanaal,* which connects Amsterdam with the North Sea, a distance of some thirty-five kilometers. We stood impatient and spellbound on the deck, absorbing the new sights and sounds, as we arrived in our motherland on April 19, 1946.

As the ship was pulled slowly through the canal by a huffing and puffing tugboat, each bridge across the canal had to be closed for the traffic on land. The Dutch people leaned on their bikes and waited for the bridge to open again. When they saw us hanging on the ship's railings, they waved their welcome to us and we waved back.

It was springtime. The light green leaves on the few weeping willow trees had just come out. The countryside was flat but fertile, and we could see for miles.

Breathlessly we gazed at the orange-colored tiled roofs of the houses on both sides of the canal and the windows that sparkled in the pale sunlight. The gardens that surrounded each home were very small but were neatly kept. Many were adorned with spring flowers.

How clean and sparkling everything looked! The air we breathed was cold and crisp and fresh. We could barely absorb it all.

When the ship was finally docked and anchored in the harbor of Amsterdam, we were met by a military band playing the Dutch national anthem, *Wilhelmus van Nassauen.* The music evoked powerful feelings in both Dutch and Indo alike. Overwhelmed and humbled, we respectfully listened to this tribute, tears flowing freely from nearly every eye. But then the thrill and the relief of having safely arrived at last in Holland took hold of us, and we "shouted for joy"!

As we disembarked, each woman received a bouquet of flowers. The men were first saluted, then either embraced or welcomed with a warm handshake.

It was so wonderful to be HOME!

Chapter Twenty-Two

Now that we were in Holland at last, our first priority was to see my father. Since he had been hospitalized in a military hospital in Soesterberg, Holland, we were transported there, where we were taken to the hostel that would be our temporary housing so we could be near him.

Soesterberg was the little town where Her Royal Highness, the Crown Princess Juliana, and her husband, Prince Bernhard, lived in the palace Soestdijk with their three children, Princess Beatrix, Irene, and Margriet, who was born in Canada during the war. Because of our loyalty to the Royal House of Orange Nassau, and Her Majesty Queen Wilhelmina and the Royal Family of the Crown Princess, we felt it appropriate that we were given the opportunity to pass their palace on our very first ride through this country, our motherland.

We did not expect to see the father we once knew. So much time had passed and conditions during the war had been so terrible. Nevertheless, we were shocked at his condition. He was so terribly thin, the result of malnutrition as well as the many diseases he had suffered. His face was distorted from cuts and a broken jaw not properly set. Just a few days previous to our arrival, he had also suffered a stroke from which he never fully recovered. As we sat beside his bed, tears of gratitude running down our faces, we could not help but notice that the nails of his fingers had been removed. We learned later they had been pulled out with bamboo slivers. His left foot had been partially chopped off to prevent a second escape from the Japanese P.O.W camp, and it had never healed properly.

But his spirits were high, and he was so pleased to see us. One by one, he held our faces in his good hand and looked us in the eyes, squeezing our cheeks, winking his eyes, and with a smile told us how grown up we had gotten. "I have waited so long for this moment," he said softly. "I love you all so very much."

We were not allowed to stay long, so reluctantly we left, waving and blowing kisses at the father we had missed so much.

In the bed next to my father lay a companion of his from the island of Ambon. His nose had rotted away, eaten up by a mixture of vinegar and hot red pepper extract that had been dripped into his nostrils while he was suspended upside down.

Many people from the island of Ambon had suffered monstrous atrocities, not only under the hands of the Japanese but also from the Indonesian revolutionists, because as faithful subjects of Queen Wilhemina they opposed the revolution. They fought with the Dutch against the Indonesians, and therefore had to flee to their motherland when Indonesia gained independence because of the severe retaliation against the people from Ambon.

My father's companion responded well to the doctors' care, and in later years he was a frequent visitor in our home.

However, my father died not long after from complications of his injuries. He was buried in an unmarked grave in Haarlem because my mother did not have the means to pay for a marker. And so the war had taken my father, my grandfather, my uncle, and my brother Herbie.

Now my mother was left alone again, with the enormous task of providing and caring for six children. She had hoped that she would be able to lean on my father to help her raise their children together. Now she had to do it alone again, this time with the additional handicap of living in a foreign country, with its unfamiliar rules and traditions, a land where Indos were considered second-class citizens by the people of Holland. She no doubt wondered where she would find the strength to go on.

As always, she turned to the Lord, putting her trust and her life in His hands.

Chapter Twenty-Three

From Soesterberg we were moved to Amsterdam, Zuid, where we were assigned by the authorities to live in the Orange Nassaulaan Number 40. This was a huge house we shared with Mrs. Vlinders, the former owner, who was under house arrest because she and her husband had been German collaborators during the war. She now lived alone, her husband having been either jailed or executed.

Mrs. Vlinders stayed in her bedroom on the second floor most of the time, coming out only to fix her meals in the kitchen. It was a strange sensation to meet her in the hallway, knowing that this house, with its rich and elaborate furnishings, once belonged to her, and now she was not even allowed to sit in any of her comfortable chairs in her own living room, because that area was assigned to our family.

As time went on, we saw less of her as she stayed in her room more and more. The few times we saw her, she was always wearing the same soiled brown dress. Although a recluse for the most part, she had an occasional good day when she would come down the stairs to offer us, from a huge box, the finest and fanciest bonbons and chocolates we had ever seen. We later found out that she had hidden hundreds of pounds of these chocolates in her wardrobe closet, and had enjoyed her chocolates and bonbons during the war while her fellow countrymen could not even get a slice of bread!

Even now, one could not go into a confectioner's store to buy 100 grams of chocolate. Sugar and chocolate were rationed, and in order to buy chocolate, it was necessary to sacrifice one's sugar allotment.

Seeing those treats made our mouths water, but we soon found out why she was so generous. The chocolates were no longer fresh, and the nuts in them were rancid. Some had lost their original color or had become white, so she wanted to get rid of them.

We lived in that house for two years, but then were forced to move because my mother could not afford the high rent. So we moved into a small three-room flat in the P.C. Hooftstraat, near the Rijksmuseum, for one-fourth of the rent Mams had been paying. However, Mams soon learned that the rent was higher than agreed upon. Twenty guilders! It was half of her weekly salary. Where would she get that kind of money for the next month?

As she had always done in times of trouble, she turned to the Lord for help. It came in a completely unexpected manner. As we were walking down the street, a man stopped her and called her by name. My mother did not know him, but he handed her an envelope and disappeared into the crowded street. When my mother opened the envelope, to her complete amazement she found one hundred guilders, enough to pay rent for the next five months!

"Quickly, child," she said as she pulled me into a side alley where she knelt and offered her thanks to God for his intervention in our behalf.

Because of the prejudice against the Indos in Holland, my mother's pharmacist certificate from the East Indies was not valid in the Netherlands. She was forced to look for other avenues of employment, and eventually found work in a small factory that manufactured patterns and transferred them to floor coverings, linens, tablecloths, and other articles ready to be hooked, crocheted, or embroidered. It was a tiresome and tedious job. After work, she hooked huge Smyrna carpets on consignment for the owner of this factory or its wealthy clients.

Many nights, Mams got very little sleep so she could meet a deadline. Her hands endlessly looped the short strings of wool, with the aid of a hook, into a tight knot through the rough material, one by one, her rhythm interrupted only when she had to count to follow the pattern or change the colors of the yarn.

Our dining table was always covered by the large rug she was currently working on. When a large piece of the rug was finished, Mams would carefully lay it out on the floor and walk on it, back and forth. "At least I have the satisfaction of being the first one to walk on this rug and to break it in," she'd say, smiling at us. Even then, Mams kept her sense of humor.

I, too, felt the prejudice in Holland as a young girl. When I went to the neighborhood butcher shop, the butcher would keep me waiting while he served everyone else in the shop, even those who entered long after I had been standing there.

"Aren't you going to help this little girl?" the last customer asked.

"I don't see anyone," the butcher, Dijkstra, said, looking directly at me. But the customer refused to be served until the butcher had helped me first.

"Why don't you help her?" he said. "You can see she has her ration coupon."

Turning reluctantly to me, the butcher said, "What do you want, you dirty little girl? "Did you even wash yourself this morning?" When I answered that of course I had done so, he replied, "Well, you certainly did not do a good job of it, because you still have dirty, brown skin!" He laughed loudly. I was humiliated.

When I returned home I told my mother, who hugged me and said, "To me you are always clean and beautiful. Remember that regardless of what others say, Heavenly Father always loves you. But for now, why don't we go to a different butcher?"

However, we also experienced love and compassion from many of the people in Holland. Our new butcher always saved the "day's special" for me as I could not come into the shop until late in the day after school. The milkman who brought our milk every other day consistently measured out the milk into our pan with an extra measure. And the green grocer a few doors down from us always had "specials" when I shopped there. While my mother worked, it was my daily task to do the shopping and prepare the evening meal. Mams would give me three guilders to buy the meat, vegetables, and bread, and she left it up to me to plan the meals.

"What will you have today?" Mr. Oudhoff would ask.

"I was thinking of endive," I said. In Holland we planned our dinner around the vegetables.

Well, I'll be," Mr. Oudhoff would grin, "I just happen to have it on special today." He would then give me one bunch more than I had money for, and I was grateful because endive would shrink when it was cooked, but I would have plenty.

And so, through the kindness of others, we managed to survive on what we had. Some years later a law was passed that would grant every war widow a modest pension, including those from the Dutch East Indies. My mother qualified for this grant, as well as for a compensation for each child under 18 years of age or older if the child attended school. This additional money was to help defray the cost of the children's shoes and clothing. It was still a struggle to make ends meet, but Konrad's earnings, combined with my mother's war widow's compensation, enabled the family to survive However, Mam's other earnings were deducted from this pension, so she decided not to work outside the home anymore. This way she could perform her motherly tasks for the children at home.

For many years on payday, Mams took the tram to the other side of the city to visit an old "Steurtje" who was even worse off than we were. She would bring her some money, flowers, and fruit, or homemade soup or a special treat, and cheer up her day with this visit. Even when we had little, my mother never failed to remember the less fortunate.

Still, life was difficult in Holland. Our two-bedroom flat was shared by the six members of our family, as Annalise had found a small studio apartment near our home. A young adult who needed her privacy, she visited occasionally, but she had her own life and her work as an x-ray technician in a large hospital kept her very busy.

Konrad became the father figure in our lives, especially after my father passed away. Before the war my father had asked Konrad to care for my mother and the family, and Konrad had accepted this role as a sacred trust.

Konrad worked as a banker in Holland, and he contributed his earnings towards our well-being. He paid the rent, took care of insurance, school supplies and books; and he even furnished me with special art supplies so I could develop my artistic talents. He bought tickets so we could attend classical concerts and plays, and he made sure there was money for school trips and visits to museums. He provided us with these "extras" until we were old enough to earn our own money for these luxuries.

Years later, when my family immigrated to the U.S., Konrad gave up his job and took a job as a postal clerk, earning much lower wages. Because he had always put my mother's welfare first, he married late in life, after Mams had retired and could take turns living with each of her children. He would live until age 59, when he would die of Lou Gehrig's disease, leaving a young wife and two daughters.

Chapter Twenty-Four

We had been living in Holland for almost a year and a half when, to my joy and surprise, I discovered my rag doll tucked away on a shelf made out of old orange crates which had been stacked one on top of another to hold our books.

Poor Pop Mientje was so dirty! She had born the brunt of my airsickness and seasickness during my voyage to Holland in both the cargo planes and on our boat trip, and now the material she was made of had begun to disintegrate.

As I reached into the stuffing to arrange it properly, my rag doll yielded up far more than the soft cotton she was made of. To my amazement, she spilled forth a treasure she had carried all these years—sapphires, diamonds, rubies, pearls, jade, and gold rings.

These were the family jewels my mother had entrusted to my nanny, Baboe Kit, before we were put under house arrest by the Japanese in the Dutch Indies. Nanny was to use them as she saw fit; they were her payment for the many years of service she had rendered to us. Perhaps the jewelry could even be used to save her own family from hunger.

After the Japanese had taken us away to our concentration camp, my nanny must have gone back to our house. There she discovered my rag doll, which in my haste I had left behind. Knowing how important my rag doll was to me, she must have devised the plan to take the larger and more valuable stones from my mother's jewelry and carefully sew them into the body and head of my rag doll. The doll she would then bring to me—an act which had cost her her life.

For seven penniless refugees living in a three-room, cold flat (a cold flat is one without central heating or hot water) in Amsterdam, the discovery of the jewels changed our entire horizon. The proceeds from the sale of the jewels eventually enabled all of us children to obtain higher education.

With this, the circle was complete. Because my parents had insisted on educating the servants alongside their children, the gift of education was returned to our family. My mother was blessed to be able to educate her children because one of her most valued servants had sacrificed her very life, knowing that one day we would be in need of the precious gift she brought to us!

Once again my mother brought the scriptures to life for me, as her charity begat charity, her mercy begat mercy, and her benevolence begat benevolence. "Therefore all things whatsoever ye would that men should do to you, do ye even so to them: for this is the law and the prophets." (Matt. 7:12.)

Chapter Twenty-Five

I was behind in my schooling, as were many other children who had spent time in concentration camps, so the Dutch government set up special classes for us called "abridgment schools." Here we would not have to attend classes with much younger children and we could advance in our schooling at our own pace. Our abridgment school combined elementary and middle school age children, and we were taught at an accelerated pace. When we had reached the level of education of our own age group, we could then transfer to the conventional public or private schools.

My class consisted of children who had been incarcerated either in Japanese or German concentration camps. Many of the students in my class were orphans who were completely alone; they had lost parents, siblings, and relatives. Many felt violated and angry; others felt indifferent about life. I was one of the latter.

One day our teacher, Mr. Simmons, took the class to Nijmegen, a town located in the far southeast corner of the province of Gelderland. It is on the banks of the river Waal, a tributary of the mighty Rhine river. An ancient city with a history dating back to the Romans, Nijmegen has always been in a very strategic position in time of war. Nijmegen and its sister-city Arnhem are the locations where the last ground battle was fought between the Allied Forces and the German troops on Dutch soil, during the winter of 1944.

Near Nijmegen is the Netherlands Allied Forces Military Cemetery, which is filled with rows and rows of small white pillar posts, bearing either the Star of David or a Latin cross and the names, ranks, and ages of those who had fallen. Some graves were identified only with a simple cross and the word "Unknown."

This field seemed miles long and miles wide. It was a sobering sight, and I can still feel the jolt in my heart when I realized how many soldiers had died—soldiers from faraway countries who had come to bring freedom. Quietly we walked past the markers, reading the names and ages of those buried there.

Mr. Simmons invited all of us to sit down in the grass. "Look at this waste of humanity," he said. "You, who are the future of this country, don't let this happen again! Commit to keeping the peace, and let peace begin with you. "We are still embroiled in a war that is not over yet. We still have boys and men fighting and dying in the Dutch Indies, right now, even as I speak. The Dutch are fighting to keep their sovereignty, the Indonesians fight for their independence. Who is right? What is right? I want you to think about this."

He then took a small booklet from the pocket of his sports jacket and read to us about another bloody war—a great war that was fought between 1861 to 1865, some eighty or so years earlier. This was the American Civil War, where the southern states fought against the northern states. In that war, too, blood brothers fought one another over issues of independence and freedom.

"I would like to read a few sentences from the 'Gettysburg Address,'" he said. "Perhaps we can glean wisdom from these words." Then he translated: "It is for us the living, rather, to be dedicated here to the unfinished work which they who fought here have thus far so nobly advanced. It is rather for us here, dedicated to the great task remaining before us—that from these honored dead we take increased devotion to that cause for which they here gave the last full measure of devotion; that we here highly resolve that these dead shall not have died in vain—that this nation, under God, shall have a new birth of freedom—and that government of the people, by the people, for the people shall not perish from the earth."

It was then, at that moment, that I decided I would always be thankful for my life. I would truly appreciate life and live a good and productive life. I would serve my God and fellowmen and not complain when things just did not go my way.

That day, Mr. Simmons showed us what it took to bring freedom to us. I realized, as I stood there in Nijmegen overlooking this seemingly endless graveyard, that these soldiers—strangers, really, to us—had shown the ultimate charity in sacrificing their lives for freedom. Our freedom.

———————————

Years later, my husband and I would visit the Netherlands American Military Cemetery in Margraten, near the city of Maastricht Holland. There a tower stands, from which the American flag proudly waves, as a monument to all those who lost their lives during this war.

In front of the tower stands a statue cast in bronze of a woman with bowed head and clasped hands, surrounded by doves. At the base of her feet is the trunk of an olive tree from which a new twig with young leaves sprouts to depict Peace. The monument bears this inscription: "In memory of the Valor and the Sacrifices which hallow this soil." On either side of the monument stands a wall that bears witness to the 1722 missing soldiers, whose remains were either never recovered or positively identified.

There are 8300 American war dead buried there, although this figure represents only 43 percent of those buried in this and other temporary cemeteries in this region alone. Of these 8300 headstones, 179 bear the Star of David, marking Jewish burials; the others are all Latin crosses, including 106 Unknowns. In no less than 40 instances, two brothers lie buried side by side, while one headstone marks the common grave of two Unknowns.

The inscription on the west side of the tower reads: "Each for his own memorial earned praise that will never die and with it the grandest of all sepulchers, not that in which his mortal bones are laid, but a home in the minds of men."

Freedom is never free. Someone must always pay the price for it, and many have paid the price to win my precious freedom.

How immensely grateful I am for the men and women in the combined Allied and American Armed Forces. I pay tribute to all of them, for it was their obedience to the laws of their country to serve, their courage and their sacrifice of life and limb and mind, that enabled me to live today, to be able to marry, to bear children, and to see my ten grandchildren grow up.

May I invoke the Lord's choicest blessings upon all the men and women who have ever served in any war, conflict, or political action, or who are now serving in the military. Our family has always been deeply grateful for the military forces—for these brave men and women who were willing to put their very lives on the line to protect the lives of others, sacrificing a period in their lives to answer the call to serve their country.

As a mother here in the United States, I have taught my children to honor our flag, to appreciate freedom, and to support and sustain the military. Our children grew up during the Vietnam era, when the majority of Americans were against this political action and turned their backs on the servicemen and women in the Armed Forces. I personally witnessed a group of young college students jeer and even spit upon their military peers when these soldiers walked out of the same plane I was waiting for. I was there to meet a couple from Texas to take them to the Oaknoll Naval Hospital in Oakland where their Marine son, who had been seriously wounded in Vietnam, had been hospitalized.

Oh, how my heart and soul cried out for justice! But all I could do was to run up to these few soldiers and welcome them home with an embrace and a kiss to ease their pain.

Another time, I took my children out of school to join the small crowd that stood on the Golden Gate Bridge, waiting to welcome home the *SS Enterprise* from a tour of duty off the Vietnam coast. We stood at the railing of the Golden Grate Bridge and admired the awesome sight of this great ship, with its cargo of choice men and women of both the Navy and Marines dressed in their white and blue dress uniforms or green utility uniforms who stood at attention on the flight decks.

No wonder this great ship was called the *Enterprise*—signifying her bold spirit and force, her courage in the face of difficulty. She radiated all of these attributes. Standing on the bridge, we threw kisses, flower petals, and confetti down to the crew below us, and they waved back to us their thanks for our support.

Oh, how I hope that we will always keep in mind the ultimate sacrifice that has been made by those who have given their lives, limbs, and even minds for our freedom, and that we will remember the display of heroism and courage of these, our honored dead as well as our honored living.

Chapter Twenty-Six

In 1949, I completed my studies at the abridgment school and was able to join the other students my age in the normal high school! How important I felt to have finally been accepted in a high school in preparation to go on to a teachers college at the university. I decided that I was going to excel in all my classes. Whatever it took, I was going to be a teacher!

In May we would have our Spring Festival, a talent night where students were invited to perform their talents. In order to appear with the festival, we had to audition and obtain the approval of a committee of school instructors. So scholastic standing also mattered a great deal.

I had begun formal piano lessons the previous fall, and one of my elective classes was to participate and play piano in the school orchestra. We met together after school hours twice a week under the direction of our teacher. Although I was not the most accomplished pianist, having had only seven months of formal lessons, we all had fun playing and listening to each other perform, so I didn't care that I was seldom chosen to play.

Then, to my complete and utter amazement, I was chosen by our teacher to play the piano part in "Blue Tango" at the Spring Festival. I practiced this piece over and over and over until I could play it by heart. Mams listened patiently as I rehearsed endlessly, the sound filling our little apartment. She praised and encouraged me, never correcting or criticizing me, just allowing me to conquer the piece at my own pace.

The festival was rapidly approaching, and rehearsals had

increased to three times a week after school to perfect our performance. We had only two weeks before our performance, and we were excited, scared, and tired. Even though preparations for this festival now had priority, we still had to finish our regular homework when we came home from rehearsals.

Our one yearly school dance was held in conjunction with the festival, so this was truly a gala affair. Some of my friends decided that since this would be our first dance, we ought to take dancing lessons!

My friend Max volunteered to contact a nearby dance studio, where we could be instructed for one guilder per lesson if we attended as a group. I didn't know where I'd find the time to go, so Max went to my home and suggested to my mother that it would "benefit me greatly." My mother laughingly concurred with Max that it was a great opportunity and learning a few dance steps would not hurt me. So what else could I do but give in and go?

Together we learned to foxtrot and to waltz, and we even learned the basic steps of the tango, samba, and rhumba. Max tried to persuade me to learn to boogie, but I thought that it would not fit my personality. I finally gave in, however, and enjoyed it tremendously.

At our rehearsal two days before festival, my friend Ina asked me, "What color is your dress going to be?"

"What dress?" I asked.

"The one you're wearing to the festival, of course," she answered, surprised that I didn't know what she was talking about. The girls around us eagerly chimed in to describe their dresses in great detail, as did Ina, while I sat silent. All these weeks I had been on cloud nine, thrilled because I had been chosen to play a solo part, and yet I had never even considered what I was going to wear that evening. I had been too worried about my performance. Now I was confronted with this dilemma.

What was I to wear? I had only three homemade skirts, two sweaters, and three blouses to my name, and none were really suitable for a dance. I did have two dresses that Tante Lien, my mother's friend, had given me. They fit nicely, and I wore them to church and to concerts and other solemn occasions. But they weren't really the kind of dresses to wear to a dance.

My bubble of happiness burst . . . what was I to do??

A deep depression came over me. I knew that my mother did not have the means of providing us with new clothes. We always received hand-me-downs, and on some occasions we might receive heavy woolen material, which my mother would sew into coats or heavy skirts. She had taught me how to alter clothes to create a new look, and I had pulled apart many old-fashioned dresses to make skirts from them. But clothes had never really been of any great concern to me—until now.

After rehearsal, I took a detour on my bike going home so I could have more time to think things over. I dallied as I rode through the Vondelpark, which I had to traverse to reach my home from school. I cried, feeling sorry for myself, thinking how unfair things were.

That evening I did not practice the piano after my homework was done. Instead, I read a book. Nor did I practice the piano the following day; and during dress rehearsal I fumbled and made mistakes on purpose, hoping that my teacher would be disgusted with me and dismiss me so I would not have to go to the festival without a pretty dress to wear.

Instead, my teacher put his hand on my shoulder and patted it a few times. "You will do well," he encouraged me. "It is a good character trait to be nervous at dress rehearsal. It shows that you are humble and not given to pride."

"We all know," he continued, "that you are blessed with a special talent. You have a gift of hearing music the way it should be played, and you are good. Remember that!" For a few moments, I forgot my dress and felt confident again.

On the day of the festival, we were dismissed early from school to give us time to get ready for the big event. Because I did not have to get ready for the evening, I took my time riding home, and let the words of my music teacher play over and over again in my mind—I was talented and had been given a special gift of music. . . .

I was blessed, I thought, and suddenly it came into my mind that I needed to thank my Heavenly Father for this gift, and for the choice opportunity I had been given to perform that night. So I got off my bike and walked to a nearby park bench, which overlooked a pretty pond. I thanked God for my life, for my fingers that could play, for my brains that could remember the music, for my eyes that could see and read music, and for my ears that I could hear.

And even though I had no pretty dress to wear to the dance, I was thankful for the chance to perform. "Bless me to play well," I prayed, "so I won't disappoint my teacher." Then I asked my Father to help me to be happy and to be content with my life.

Even as I was praying, I suddenly felt as if the heaviness and sadness were taken off my shoulders, and I felt "light" and happy and cheerful.

I remained seated on the bench for a while, enjoying the serenity and beauty around me. It was springtime, some trees were in bloom, and I realized how beautiful the world around me was. I had a lot to be thankful for. How peaceful the park was with no one around, and I giggled as I watched some little ducks in the pond following their mother, swimming vigorously and trying to keep up with her.

I made my decision: the lack of a new dress was not going to spoil my big event! After all, I said to myself, one shouldn't judge a book by its cover, and what's inside a person is more valuable than what the person looks like on the outside. I decided that I would wear the blue and black dress from Tante Lien, which would look distinguished. Only a very few people would know that this dress was a hand-me-down.

After the performance, I would sit with my mother and sister and watch the others dance and listen to the music. That would be just as much fun and maybe next year I would be able to get a dress suitable for a dance. *I can wait*, I told myself.

By the time I reached home, I had fully reconciled myself with the decision to be happy and to remain cheerful. I raced up the stairs to our apartment and found my mother dressed in her nice dress, and wearing stockings and shoes, as if she was planning to go out somewhere.

"There you are at last," she said. "Come here and drink your tea, then let us go."

"Where are we going?" I asked.

"I read in the paper about a fabric store that has pretty material on sale. We are going to take a look there and see what we can buy. Every piano soloist who is to perform at a school festival deserves a pretty new dress, something light and springy. Don't you agree?"

I was utterly amazed! Somehow my mother had known how important a new dress was to me. I stared at her, speechless, and she took my face into her hands and kissed me. Oh, how I loved my mother! How I admired her calm wisdom and insight into my heart. What a wonderful surprise. I did not have to wait until next year to get my dress!

As I drank my tea, I wondered how a mother knows what goes on in her child's mind and heart. Was it because they themselves were young girls once, or did God talk to mothers about their children? Did He show mothers what to do? And how could my mother afford this material, I wondered. What did she go without to have the money to buy material for a new dress?

I looked at my mother and thanked her. She smiled at me and said, "I am so proud of you, *Ittepetit*. You worked hard at this piano piece, and you deserve something new to wear for the concert.

"Tante Lien sent me some money, which arrived in this morning's mail. We will use this to buy material for a new dress for you.

"You look good in pink," my mother said. "When you were a little girl, Baboe Kit liked to dress you in pink. Would you like a pink dress?"

We had bought enough material to make the kind of dress I had seen once—one with a square neck and a flared skirt with a ribbon in the back. There would also be enough to make a beautiful bow in the back and a ribbon for my hair.

At home, Mams immediately went to work on the dress, draping the material around me, taking my measurements, then carefully cutting the material on the table.

At six o'clock my beautiful new dress was ready, with its square neck and flared skirt with a ribbon in the back that tied into a bow. Oh, what a beautiful dress!

I tried on my new dress and it fit perfectly. I started to cry, and Mams hugged me and pulled me close to her. "None of this now, you need to look beautiful tonight and your eyes need to sparkle."

Mams and I hemmed the dress together. Each of us started at the opposite side of the dress, making careful, tiny stitches, and meeting where the other had started to stitch.

While Mams had been sewing, my sister Ellen and I fixed dinner.

We ate quickly, then took the tram to the school festival, which was held at the Krasnapolski, a large hotel downtown.

Truly, I felt like Cinderella on her way to the ball. The dress felt so soft, and it smelled brand new. With my white socks and my shoes nicely polished, I knew I looked good. Once again I was in seventh heaven. I felt I could conquer any obstacle, even the fear of performing before a large audience and my peers.

At the hotel, I was directed to the backstage to check in and receive last minute instructions. My schoolmates admired my dress, and I could see that some were surprised to see me in a brand new dress.

Of course my teacher made it a point to give a compliment on the way I looked. "Your pretty eyes sparkle and your face glows," he said. My spirits soared!

Just before I was due to go on stage, I remembered to say a little prayer, to thank my Heavenly Father for hearing my prayers and solving my problems. "Thank you for letting me be part of this evening. Help me to remember my part." I felt a peaceful feeling come over me.

When I sat down at the big black grand piano in the middle of the stage, I saw my mother nod her head to encourage me. And so I played for her.

Afterwards, as I stood on stage acknowledging the applause that followed, it felt so good to know that my mother and my music teacher were proud of me. I knew also that Heavenly Father was proud of me.

Now I could relax and join my mother and sister in the audience to enjoy the other performances. There were prose and poetry readings, excerpts from serious and comic plays, dancers and singers, acrobats and jugglers, and even an exposition of the martial arts.

At the dance following the festival, I felt like the belle of the ball, even though I sat by my mother, mostly watching people dance until Scott Baun, a third-year student, came up and asked me to dance. My friends and I had always looked up to the upperclassmen, and here was one of the handsomest upperclassmen asking me to dance!

Ellen grinned at me from behind Scott Baun's back as we walked to the dance floor. I was grateful for the few dancing lessons I had, thanks to Max's insistence, so I would not feel foolish and helpless on the dance floor with such a handsome upperclassman.

After that the dance was wonderful! I was asked to dance many times, which was a surprise, as I had always considered myself an ugly duckling.

In between dances, I shared a treat of real Coca-Cola with Ellen while Mams had a cup of coffee. "Stay and dance," my mother urged me when the clock struck ten. "I'll take Ellen home." Max assured my mother that he personally would take me home on his bike, so I would not have to take the tram alone so late in the evening.

What a wonderful dance! I danced with all my friends as well as with several of the upperclassmen. I was so flattered by their attention, and felt I knew exactly how Cinderella must have felt when she was able to go to the ball in her new dress.

Even amidst the laughter and the music, as I danced I kept thanking my Heavenly Father for giving me such a wonderful, sweet mother, who was so sensitive to her children's needs, that she provided me with a beautiful pink dress. I thanked Him for Tante Lien, for her generosity and kindness and for remaining such a true friend to my mother throughout the years.

And I thanked Him for answering my prayers, for knowing my innermost thoughts and letting me know that I was indeed important to Him. I felt truly that I was a daughter of God.

Chapter Twenty-Seven

Each year during Christmas vacation, the high schools in Amsterdam held their tournaments to compete against each other in different sports and other events. There were competitions in the arts as well as in sports. We had volleyball and basketball playoffs, gymnastics, martial arts, and water sports such as swimming, diving, and water polo. In the arts there were competitive piano recitals, light opera, prose and poetry readings, and art exhibitions in painting and sculpting. The school bands and choirs challenged each other for the best performances.

It was my senior year and I was dating Gerard, the captain of our school basketball team. That was the year I met Bob.

Bob had transferred from another school and had been elected an officer in the student body. He was very outgoing and handsome, but I thought he was too boisterous and loud for me.

Bob was put in charge of selling the tickets for the tournament. For some reason I was late getting my ticket, and as I stood in line I heard that there were only a few left.

I reached the front of the line and there was Bob selling the tickets. He looked up at me, waved a ticket in the air, and said, "I'll let you have this last ticket under one condition—that you let me pay for it, and I'll pick you up at 7:00 p.m. Monday for the opening swimming meet."

I was horrified! "You know I'm dating Gerard," I said. In fact, Bob played guard on the very same team with Gerard! "You can keep the ticket. I don't need it that badly," I said as I stomped away. How dare he think I could be manipulated into going out with him!

I told Gerard about this incident, but he merely laughed it off.

"Bob's harmless," he said. "He's all talk and no show! Why don't you take the ticket and go with him. You don't want to miss this event, and I have to work Monday. You know you're crazy about the water sports."

I did want to go, but I was irritated to see Gerard so nonchalant about this whole thing. Didn't he care if I went out with another boy?

The next day, as I was walking in the crowded school hall to my Dutch literature class with my girlfriend Meta, I heard Bob bellowing behind us, "Hey, Kitty, don't we have a date? I have your ticket!" And there was Bob, waving the ticket in the air, grinning.

"What's this all about?" Meta asked. I told her the story, expecting her to sympathize with me.

"How exciting! You are going, aren't you? Imagine two guys wanting to date you at the same time! And Bob is so much more handsome than Gerard, if you ask me," she said impishly.

"I did *not* ask you, Meta," I replied, "and I am not going, thank you very much."

"You will regret it!" Meta teased as she walked on to her history class.

I had three class periods to make my decision. Should I miss the whole tournament because of my pride? Then again, maybe Bob was just teasing. But if Gerard didn't seem to care if I went with Bob, why should I feel guilty? Gerard and I were just friends who happened to be dating each other.

Bob and I had a geography class together in fifth period. I had decided to compromise and accept only part of the bargain, because I really did want to go. But every time I looked up and caught Bob's eye, he grinned at me. It was so irritating! He was so sure of himself!

Just because of that, I decided to play it "cool." I would wait until school was over before I let Bob know what I had decided.

After school, I walked to the bike rack to get my bike to go home, when I noticed Bob walking towards me from the opposite direction.

"Hey, pretty dark girl, here is your ticket!" He grinned and handed me the ticket. "You can have it. I was only teasing the other day, but I'd really like to take you to the games. What do you say?"

I looked at him. Maybe he was not such a bad choice after all.

His approach was certainly unique! It could be interesting. And I did like his eyes!

"You can pick me up at 6:30 p.m. Monday, because I want to be there early. But I am paying for my own ticket," I retorted.

"It's a deal!" he smiled. "You're okay," he said and gave me the "thumbs up" sign. "I'll see you Monday, then." He walked away whistling.

Relieved, I put the coveted ticket in my wallet—but not before I noticed that instead of writing my name on the ticket, Bob had written *Lief Zwartje* ("Sweet little dark girl"). He was incorrigible!

As a young girl I had been called many unflattering names like "Peanut Chinese," or "Blackhead," or "Chocolate doll." But I knew those names had been meant to hurt me. I considered the name Bob had called me as a compliment.

Promptly at 6:30 p.m. Monday, Bob rang the doorbell of the apartment to pick me up. He was clean shaven and smelled like Palmolive soap.

Unbeknownst to me, the previous day had been his birthday and his parents had given him a brand new, three-speed bike. It was the top of the line brand and a beautiful bicycle. "Well, congratulations and belated happy birthday," I said. "You should have told me, I would have gotten you something."

"No need for that!" he answered. "To spend the evening with you is all I wanted for my birthday!"

We would ride together on his new bike to the competition, and he indicated that I should sit "side saddle" on the bar of his bike instead of on the luggage rack in back. This meant that I had to lean against his chest and he had to hold me steady. I rode "in his arms" all the way to the other side of town where the swim meet was held.

Bob proved to be a real gentleman. He was so interesting to talk to, and I found that we liked many of the same things. He was very intelligent and humorous. Beneath his veneer of bravura was a gentle, kind, and thoughtful young man. I decided that I liked Bob very much.

Three days later, Bob brought me home after the basketball playoffs. Our school had won three out of four games, and the other members of the basketball team were exhausted but wanted to stay to watch their competition. I had already watched all four games, which took almost all day, and now I needed to get home. I wanted to change my clothes because at six o'clock I was expected to attend a typing class at a private school named Schoevers, at the Van Baerlestraat, just around the corner from my house.

I thought it strange that Gerard did not offer to take me home, but I enjoyed Bob's company so I did not question it further. It had started to rain, and Bob and I decided to walk our bikes instead of riding them. As we walked along, we talked and talked.

Then, just before we turned the corner into my street, Bob leaned over suddenly and kissed me, there in the drizzling rain, in front of the show window of the Van Meeuwens, in the VanderVeldestraat, around the corner from my house. It was Wednesday, December 23, 1953.

I learned later from Bob that he told Gerard he could take me away from him. Gerard bet him that I could not be persuaded. But Gerard lost!

Chapter Twenty-Eight

Bob wanted to attend college; however, because he had failed some of his high school classes, he did not graduate and so could not study at the university. His parents would not allow him to repeat his failed classes because they wanted him to go to work. Bob was inconsolable.

I desperately wanted to help him, but the only way I knew was to pray for him. I knew too that the only one who could help Bob was our Heavenly Father. I knew he could heal my friend Bob's wounds of pain, sorrow, and regret. "Bob," I suggested one night, "why don't we pray about this?"

Bob had never prayed before, and I was honored to show him how. We went into the tiny kitchen in my mother's small apartment for privacy, knelt down in front of the garbage container, and clasped our hands together in prayer. Humbly I asked Heavenly Father to bless my friend Bob, to grant him a second chance, to open a door so that he could continue his education.

In that instant Bob felt vividly that there was a God, and he was greatly comforted.

After this sacred experience, we decided to talk to my mother and to ask her advice. She listened intently, then asked Bob what he wanted to study. He wanted to be a teacher, he said. She considered the situation and agreed to take matters into her hands.

First, she asked Bob's parents' permission to intercede in their son's behalf, then she arranged a meeting with the director of the teachers college at the university to discuss Bob's dilemma.

It took several visits and a great deal of diplomacy, pleading, and explaining, but at last she was able to obtain the director's consent for Bob to take an entrance examination to qualify to study at the university. He passed with flying colors!

Bob and I began to go to church together. He felt ill at ease in the Protestant Koepelkerk near our home where our family was registered to worship, so we began to explore. We went to various churches of different denominations although as Protestants we naturally did not attend the Roman Catholic church.

Religion was very important to me. I had made it a habit to pray at least twice a day, as I found that I needed the comfort of communicating with Deity. I found that if I kept open the communication lines with heaven, in time of need or even in time of rejoicing I could draw on the powers of heaven.

Bob and I were acquainted with the Mormon church through our classes at school, which required a study of the religions of the world. Our classroom debates were usually very academic and sterile, without compassion or conviction for a particular belief. The majority of students considered themselves too sophisticated and practical to have to deal with religion, let alone practice it. Mormonism had been discussed with a great deal of negative feeling because of the practice of taking plural wives and also because the majority of the class considered Mormonism as a cult rather than a belief.

One student, Joke Bertram, spoke up in their defense. She knew a Mormon family, she said, and had learned firsthand that these Mormons lived by a strict health code and adhered to a high moral standard. They also believed in modern-day prophecy.

Bob and I were also aware of another religion, one in which everyone was a saint, as we passed its church every day on the way to the college. The church stood across the Rijksmuseam and bore the strange name of "The Church of Jesus Christ of Latter-day Saints." We did not connect this church to the Mormon religion

"The members of this church must think highly of themselves to elevate themselves to be called 'Saints,'" I said to Bob. "What a responsibility and what an effort it must take to behave like a 'Saint' all the days of your life. I am glad that I am a common Protestant."

Bob and I finally decided to attend the Scottish Anglican church, where the services were conducted in English. The clergyman was a

Scott from Edinborough, who spoke with a Scottish accent.

The church was located in the heart of the city in *het Begijnhof*, which used to be an ancient convent dating back to the twelfth century. The buildings were surrounded by a thick wall, which kept out the everyday noises of the busy world outside. The whole area radiated peace.

We were welcomed with open arms, and I felt very comfortable. Later Konrad and the whole family joined us in worshipping at the Scottish church, mostly to familiarize themselves with the spoken English language, which we had studied from textbooks but still had difficulties with. We considered it another hour of education, as we learned to be more fluent in the English language by mingling with the British and Dutch congregation.

Chapter Twenty Nine

Under President Dwight D. Eisenhower, special visas were extended to all survivors of concentration camps to come to America if they so desired. My mother so desired! She was even willing to start a new life all over again in the U.S. at the age of fifty-five, even if she had to work in a steel factory to make a living.

Her youngest brother John and his family were already living in America, which had not been an unfamiliar country for him since he had received his military training in Arizona with the U.S. Air Force during World War II. He had fallen in love with this country and jumped at the chance to emigrate. He and his wife, my Aunt Cora, were sponsored by the North Methodist Church in Manchester, Connecticut, so they settled there until they became independent from their sponsors.

In Holland, we were still considered second-class citizens, and Mams knew that America would free us from the limitations we faced in Holland and grant us the liberty and the opportunity to become whatever we wanted to become, as long as we were willing to work hard for the things we desired.

Mother also had another reason to go: America had diplomatic relations with the Indonesian government, which Holland did not then have. Perhaps she hoped that in the future, some restitution would be made to our family by Indonesia for our confiscated properties. However, this would have to be resolved through diplomatic relations and would need the assistance of the U.S. to exert some pressure on Indonesia.

Mams was convinced that it would be in the best interest of all her children to immigrate to America, even though we were already well established in the Dutch community. My brother Konrad had a prestigious and satisfying position with the Algemene Nederlandse Handels Bank. Annalise was married, and she and her husband had a small child and a comfortable life. Daniel was engaged to a lovely Indo teacher, and he was employed as a tool and die maker and made a good living. Ellen and Wim were high school students, and I was just finishing my teacher's certificate in college.

I struggled with the decision whether or not to move. I knew Mams' deepest wish was for her children to have a new life in America. Although my brothers and sisters were willing to move and begin a new life, I was not convinced that this move would be best for me.

At last I confided in my mother and explained to her my fears and apprehension about this move. "I feel as if my whole being is split in two parts," I told her. "Part of me cries out that I want to stay here in Holland to be a teacher. You know this has been my life-long ambition, and I've worked so hard and studied so hard to achieve this goal, and I am now so close. How can I possibly change my course now, in the middle of the stream? And what can America possibly offer me more than that what I already have here?"

Mams listened patiently and I continued. "The other part pleads with me to follow your wishes. You know that I don't want to cause you sorrow, and that means I have to go where you want me to go. Tell me, Mams, why is it so important that I go to America?" She didn't answer, and I said the one thing that was on both our minds. "Then, too, there is Bob. I would have to leave him behind."

Mams held me and said, "My child, you are the only one who can solve this problem. You need to work it out in your heart, make a decision, then ask the Lord if it is a good decision.

"All I can tell you is that I know that we have to go to America. I have a feeling that it is of great importance for us to take this opportunity to emigrate. Are you aware that the waiting list for Asian-born people like us for visas is so long that it could take up to fifteen years to process?" I shook my head.

"Now look at us today. This visa is being given to us on a silver platter. I truly feel this is a gift from God. We have to go, we must go. My child, go ask of the Lord. He will tell you what you must do."

I did not have to ask the Lord; I knew what I had to do. I had to follow my family to America. They needed me, as I was the most proficient in the English language. And I knew Mams would only be happy with all her children under her wings.

Reluctantly I went through the motions to get my papers in order to obtain my visa. As part of the extensive screening process necessary to obtain a permanent residency visa for the U.S., all our civil papers—our birth certificates, diplomas, etc.—had to be translated from Dutch into English and then notarized for their authenticity. We had to have full medical clearance and also needed to be inoculated again against tuberculosis, DPT, and other diseases. We even had to have our teeth checked!

We applied for passports, filled out numerous forms, and endured endless interrogations by the American Immigration officers at the American Consulate who wanted to know everything about us.

Once again we had to sort through our belongings and decide what would come with us and what we would sell or leave behind. I felt this a doubly traumatic experience because my heart was not into this move.

During this chaotic time, a cleaning woman threw out my still-cherished rag doll. She did not realize how precious this old and dirty "rag" was to me for all its memories, and she had given it to a ragman. I was devastated at this particular loss. My rag doll was all I had left of my childhood.

Chapter Thirty

I arrived with my family at the Idylwild Airport, now called JFK Airport, in New York City on March 25, 1957, to begin a new life in America.

As we had expected, Bob could not come to America with us as he did not qualify for this special visa. He remained in Holland and finished his schooling; after graduation he taught school in Holland, which he thoroughly enjoyed.

We wrote each other long letters, and he tried to persuade me to come back to Holland. He had applied for a visa but it was a long, slow process, further delayed by the Dutch government until the deferment of his military obligation had been absolved. He was so very unhappy, and I was unhappy knowing that he was unhappy. We finally decided that we should marry, and were married by proxy. My brother Daniel stood in for Bob at the Dutch Consulate in New York on October 2, 1957; Daniel's fiancée, Dea, who was still in Holland, stood in for me with Bob in Amsterdam on November 18, 1957.

It was not until January 6, 1959, that Bob was able to join us in America. But there was an important reason for the two-year delay. While Bob was waiting in frustration for his visa, two Mormon missionaries tracked down the Admiralengracht in Amsterdam and knocked on the door of my husband's parents' home.

Bob was teaching school, but his mother invited the missionaries to come back when he would be home. She knew that Bob would be interested to hear about their religion.

The missionaries returned and presented to him the plan of salvation. Bob wrote to me that when he heard the plan of salvation, its truth enlightened his mind and his vision enlarged. He wanted to be baptized.

However, at that time, missionaries did not challenge their investigators to baptism until they had taught them for quite a while. The missionaries wanted Bob to come to several church meetings and other church activities, become familiar with the various church programs, and have time to feel at ease. And so Elders Andrus and Thurgood taught him for several months. One day they invited Bob to have dinner with them and introduced him to the American hamburger and he was hooked for life! (When he came to the United States, we could never pass the "Golden Arches" without stopping for a hamburger!)

Bob was baptized into The Church of Jesus Christ of Latter-day Saints on November 28, 1958, in the very same church building across the Rijksmuseum that he and I used to pass by and wonder about.

I was thrilled with his enthusiastic letter describing his baptism in the Mormon church. Although I still knew little about the Mormons, I was happy that Bob had found direction and purpose in his life again. His despondency had left him. He longed to come to America and to start a brand new life here.

I looked heavenward and thanked my Heavenly Father for sending these missionaries to my husband. But then I stopped and asked, "But why, Lord, did it have to be the Mormon church, of all the churches in this world?!" The only knowledge I had of the Mormons was that they lived by a strict health code and adhered to high moral standards, which I had no problem with. What did concern me was that most Mormons lived in or were required to come to live in some godforsaken country called Utah, and I had no desire to live there. The Mormons might call Utah their "Zion," but it sounded like an awful place to me—bland and dreary, desolate and overgrown with sage brush. I had heard that the summers were hot and the winters were cold, a typical desert climate that did not appeal to me at all.

But what disturbed me most of all was the fact that Mormon men had more than one wife, and I was not quite ready to share my brand new husband with another wife. So I wrote to ask Bob to please wait to procure another wife until he had seen me again.

Bob wrote quickly to explain that this commandment had been withdrawn by the Lord through modern-day revelation to his prophet, who leads the Church on this earth. The people no longer practiced polygamy. I would always be his Number One wife, Bob assured me, now and forever. "I have loved you from the very first moment that I saw you walking down the halls of the high school," he wrote. "I determined then and there that you would be my sweetheart and wife, the mother of my children."

The most difficult part of Mormonism for me to accept was that Joseph Smith was a prophet of God. I could not understand why a mere fourteen-year-old boy had been chosen by the Lord to be privileged to receive a visit from God the Father and Jesus Christ.

Furthermore, I had always been taught that the Lord did not use prophets any more and the only communication with heaven was through personal revelation, through dreams or through inspiration, as I had witnessed it in my mother's life.

Still, when Bob finally came to the U.S., I consented to attend church with him; and for two years I investigated the Church. I found the members to be very warm and congenial, and I liked how they called each other brother and sister.

The church was thirty miles away and we did not own a car. Transportation by bus was not available during those hours on a Sunday. And so every Sunday somebody from the church would pick us up for Sunday School classes in the morning and take us home afterwards. A member would also pick us up in the afternoon for sacrament services and bring us home again afterwards. In addition, our faithful home teacher drove the eighty-mile round trip to visit us each month to give us a gospel message and to inquire about our welfare. We felt so loved by all the members.

The missionaries also came to visit us frequently. One missionary, Elder Ralph Carpenter, from Salt Lake City, set out to convert me. He suggested that I study the Book of Mormon and the other scriptures, in addition to the Holy Bible. He and his companion visited us two and three times a week to encourage me in my studies.

As I read the Book of Mormon, I came upon a passage that had been taught to me as a child by my uneducated nanny: "For it must needs be, that there is an opposition in all things. . . . even the forbidden fruit in opposition to the tree of life; the one being sweet and the other bitter." (2 Ne. 2:11, 15.)

How many times had Baboe Kit reminded me, when things did

not go well or did not turn out to be what I expected, "There has to be opposition in all things. We have to taste of the bitter to savor the sweet things in life."

As a young girl I had asked my nanny once, "Where do I come from?" I had already dismissed the tales about "storks bringing babies" and "babies being found in a cabbage patch." I wanted to know where I really came from. I knew that my body was formed in my mothers belly, but I felt that I must have come from somewhere before this.

A sweet smile had come over her face as she drew me close to her. "Once upon a time," she said, "you and I and all the people in this world lived on the courts on high with God. Our spirits were born there. Then we came on earth to live, through earthly parents."

Baboe Kit told me many stories, and I listened to them with fascination or perhaps even recognition. She told me mysterious stories about a big and brave man who had come from lands far away where the sweet potato grows. He was very adventurous and built a mighty ship. Many people were eager to come with him, so they left their homes to go on this adventure. The trade winds took them far away from their country and they eventually landed in these beautiful islands. He was called Hagata or Hakate, and he became king of people on the islands. He was a good king. As I now read the Book of Mormon, I discovered a familiar story in Alma 63:5-8.

> And it came to pass that Hagoth, he being an exceedingly curious man, therefore he went forth and built him an exceedingly large ship . . . and launched it forth into the west sea, by the narrow neck which led into the land northward.
>
> And behold, there were many of the Nephites who did enter therein and did sail forth with much provisions, and also many women and children. . . .
>
> And it came to pass that they were never heard of more. And we suppose that they were drowned in the depths of the sea. And it came to pass that one other ship also did sail forth; and whither she did go, we know not.

All these years I had considered these truths to be part of my nanny's belief, and now I found these teachings recorded in the Book of Mormon. Oh, how great was my joy to find that these truths also belonged to the restored gospel of Jesus Christ!

I could not put down this sacred book. I devoured its contents, and for the first time I felt as if the ancient prophets were actually speaking to me from the dust.

When my sweet husband took me on my first trip back to Java to the land where I was born, which I had left some forty-eight years earlier, we decided to take a tour through middle Java, making Solo our home base because of its central location.

There, east of Solo, in the middle of the island of Java, in the small village of Tawang Mangu, stands a Sukuh temple dating back from before 500 A.D. It is built in the same pyramid shape as the Mayan temples found in the lands of the Book of Mormon. It has steep stairs leading up to three different levels.

The native Indonesians call this the temple of the "unknown religion." They have no records of who built it or to what religion this temple belongs. Many original parts have been destroyed, or have been taken away. First, the Buddhists added some carved reliefs to the base of the temple adapting it to a place of worship for their religion. When the Buddhists were driven out of middle Java to the East, this temple was taken over by the Hindus, who used it for their religion. They, in turn, transformed it into a place of learning the art of loving, where the priests would teach young women the art of love.

At the base of the temple are three turtles, a symbol of the Hindu religion, surrounded by many statues, some erotic in nature. One in particular depicts an ovary, where the gods determine on which side of the ovary the egg will be fertilized. If it is fertilized on the right side, the person created will be a good person with a strong character, wanting to do good and follow the gods. If the egg is fertilized on the left side, the character of the person created will be flawed and subject to evil impulses, as it will have the tendency to follow and serve the evil one.

When the Muslims finally took over the country, they defaced all statues by chopping off their heads, because Allah is their god and Mohammed his prophet, and the worship of God through images is forbidden.

I was fascinated as our guide explained these religions, which have so much in common with beliefs held by Latter-day Saints. For example, many believe in the three degrees of glory, our pre-earth existence, and the coming of the Messiah, who was born of an earthly mother although his father was a god. Some teach of the tree of life and the necessity for conflict between good and evil. Many religions teach that one must struggle to perfect one's character, to avoid unrighteous dominion, to overcome the desire for power and wealth and live a simple life of charity and integrity.

Isn't this what the pure gospel of Jesus Christ is all about?

This was the heritage my nanny and my own mother passed on to me. No wonder, then, that I was attracted and converted to the restored gospel of Jesus Christ when it was presented to me some 33 years ago.

Chapter Thirty-One

I investigated the Church for two years. As I studied the scriptures, I had the sensation that a veil was being lifted from my eyes. I began to see clearly. My understanding deepened, and the messages from our prophets, seers, and revelators registered in my ears. I understood at last that Joseph Smith was indeed a prophet of God and had been chosen and set apart when he was only fourteen years old, before he could be tainted by worldly influences, and groomed by God to become His prophet.

I realized that this was not strange, as the Lord had called other prophets at an early age before, such as Samuel and Daniel. The Lord Jesus Christ Himself taught the rabbis and the elders of Israel in the temple in Jerusalem when He was only twelve years old.

At the admonition of the missionaries, I knelt down on my knees and asked my Heavenly Father to let me know if I should believe that Joseph Smith was a prophet of God and accept the Book of Mormon as another witness of the Lord Jesus Christ.

A warm feeling came over me, a feeling of well-being, of joy, and of peace. Then I knew, as I now know, that this is the restored gospel of Jesus Christ.

I requested baptism and was interviewed by the assistant to the mission president of the area. I was intrigued by the pin that the assistant wore, which was unlike the golden question marks that other missionaries wore to invite people to ask the "golden questions."

This elder wore in his lapel a pin with the letters "L.D.S."

"What does that mean?" I asked. "And why do you wear this?"

He answered, "These letters stand for Latter-day Saints. You are about to be baptized into The Church Of Jesus Christ of Latter-day Saints—the Mormon church or the L.D.S. church."

Suddenly a picture came into my mind of a time that I wanted to forget, and I remembered that I had seen this insignia many years ago on a dying American soldier who had worn dog tags with the initials L.D.S. He had told us of his belief in this American church, and asked my mother to look for it if she ever came to America.

I had never realized that this new church into which I was about to be baptized was also known as the L.D.S. church! I knew it only as the Mormon church or The Church of Jesus Christ of Latter-day Saints. My "brothers" and "sisters" in my Hartford branch called themselves Mormons or Saints, but I had never made the connection. And of course in Dutch, the name of the Church does not have these initials, so I had never made the connection in Holland.

When I phoned my mother to tell her that I wanted to be baptized into the Mormon Church, she remained silent. "Can we talk about this before you do this?" she asked.

We made an appointment to meet after work, and I walked to the hospital where she worked. As Bob and I did not live far from there, I invited her to come to the apartment where we could talk in private. There we had a long, heart-to-heart talk.

Mams told me that she had known years ago what L.D.S. stood for, because the Mormon missionaries in Holland had come to our apartment to ask her permission to baptize my youngest brother, Wim, who had become involved in the scouting program sponsored by the Mormon church in Amsterdam. She had not given them permission, saying that Wim was too young to know what church to choose. After that, she had not made any inquiries about the Church as she did not want anything to do with it.

I told her how I felt about the Church and what the Church believed, but Mams nonetheless advised me against joining. "Our religion is the Dutch Reformed church, a Protestant denomination," she said. "Our family has been sponsored by the Congregational church here in town. Don't you understand that you are showing ingratitude to our sponsors if you defect to another church, especially a church with no affiliation to the Protestants?"

I could tell that my mother was worried and distraught. Suddenly she looked old and tired. I tried to comfort her.

"Mams, I have been investigating this church for almost two years now. I have not been going to the Congregational church. And you know the Reverend Simpson and I did not see eye to eye on different issues," I answered.

"Yes, I know," she said. "I want you to know that I did not agree with him either. He should have had more charity. But I will remind you that faith in our God and the scriptures from the Holy Bible pulled us through many hard times. I have often felt the Lord's love encircle me. So I know our religion is not wrong."

I tried to explain. "Mams, in the Mormon church we believe that the pure and authentic gospel of Jesus Christ has been tampered with over the past 1900-plus years. Some truths have been taken away, and other ideas have been added to it. Just think how many times the Holy Bible has been translated—you can imagine how many pure and precious things have been translated incorrectly!

"Mams, I know that Joseph Smith has been called and ordained a prophet of God. Over a period of several years, the angel Moroni, who was one of the prophets of the Lord in Book of Mormon times, taught him the restored gospel. No, Mams, your religion isn't wrong, but it isn't the complete gospel of Jesus Christ. Doesn't it make sense that I would like to have the pure religion and follow its teachings?"

Somehow I had to make her understand. "Remember when you and I went shopping in Holland, we always looked for the 'real' things. We would rather have less of the 'real' thing than more of the false. For example, for the same money we could buy two pounds of surrogate coffee, the coffee mixed with grain, but we always preferred the real coffee ground from coffee beans. For that money we could only buy one pound of the real thing, so we had to be content with less, but we knew we had the real thing."

"It was the same thing with horse meat versus beef. We preferred the real ground beef, in much lesser quantity, over a large quantity of ground horse meat, for the same amount of money. Some people might call it arrogance or stupidity, but it's neither. It showed that we had 'class,' and a child of God should have 'class.' Remember, you always said that, Mams.

"So now I would rather have the real gospel—the restored gospel—in my life. Can you understand that, Mams? I have discovered the 'real' thing, and because I am a daughter of God, I want to show that I have 'class.' And no matter what anybody thinks of me, I need to follow the dictates of my conscience and be baptized into the Mormon church."

Never before had I spoken so frankly with my mother. I did not know where the words came from, but I felt valiant. I sensed that Mams was disappointed in me, which made me sad because she did not understand.

On July 17, 1961, I entered into the waters of baptism in West Hartford, Connecticut, and became a member of The Church of Jesus Christ of Latter-day Saints.

From the time that Bob had received the blessings of the Melchezidek priesthood, it was our desire to go to the temple of the Lord to receive our endowments and temple blessings. We put all of our extra change into a large glass container to save for our trip to Utah, which was the nearest temple to our home in Connecticut.

One day Bob called me from work. The conversation did not start the usual way, rather, he began to whistle the tune "San Francisco here we come!"

"What is this all about?" I asked. "It means that you, the children, and I are going to live in the San Francisco area. I'm being transferred!"

I knew what Bob was saying. San Francisco was close to Oakland and Oakland had a temple! Our deepest wish had been fulfilled! Five and one-half years after I was baptized, on February 4, 1967, my dear husband and I were sealed for time and all eternity in the Oakland temple.

Chapter Thirty-Two

The first year after my baptism we endured unemployment and lay-offs, and it was necessary to move, first to East Hartford, and later to Bristol. Perhaps for this reason, my mother did not visit our home for almost two years. When we could afford the gas money, I took the children to see their grandmother, which of course she enjoyed. However, our conversations were never quite the same as before I had joined the Church. This was, perhaps, because my life was completely immersed with the Church and all our friends were members of the Church. All our experiences were connected with the Church, and Mams did not want me to talk about the Church.

I did manage, however, to tell her about some events in our lives, which proved how dedicated and truly loving the members of our little branch were. They truly loved us as the Lord loves us, and they strengthened our faith. At this time Bob was working at Friendly Ice Cream, a creamery and sandwich shop franchise, in their management training program. He was required to work on two Sundays a month, which meant that he could not attend church.

One day our branch president came to visit Bob and challenged him to find other employment. Bob was needed at church. "The Lord will bless you," the branch president said, "and you will never go without."

Without hesitation, Bob quit his job at Friendly and started work as a house painter for a counselor in the branch presidency, Brother Green. But when winter came, Bob was laid off.

During an especially difficult time, I looked at my shelves one day and saw that all I had was two bottles of baby food. I gave one to three-year-old Scott, who then asked, "Can I have a sandwich, Mother?"

I had to tell him, no, we had no bread for a sandwich and no money to buy the bread. Some time later he stood before me, a loaf of bread in his arms.

"Where on earth did you get that bread?" I asked. "At the store," he said. I realized that my three-year-old son had walked down the stairs, crossed the street, and walked to the store all by himself! On top of that he had told the grocer that we needed bread!

"We need to take it back," I told him. "We can't pay for it." We walked to the store, but to my surprise, the grocer shook his head when I tried to return it. "Just pay me when you can," he said.

It was 1961, and we lived in a small two-bedroom apartment on the third floor with only a space heater to keep us warm. The winter was bitter cold and on the day that the kerosene ran out I had no money to buy more. So I covered the windows with newspaper to help keep the cold out, then moved our children into our tiny kitchen where I lit the gas stove burners and oven for heat. One could say that it was even very cozy there!

Presently the front doorbell rang, and there stood my two visiting teachers who had driven at least 15 miles to see me. I was completely embarrassed to have them see my situation but I invited them to come into our kitchen with us. As is the Dutch custom, I offered them a warm drink of cocoa, which they did not want; however, my two children did. I heated some water, as we had no milk, and mixed the cocoa in it then gave it to the children to drink. After my visiting teachers gave me their message and we exchange pleasantries, they left. Despite the momentary embarrassment, I was inspired by their message and although it was cold, I felt warm inside.

That afternoon, just before Bob came home from looking for work, the branch president came by. He measured the walls for pipes then left. A few hours later he returned with one of the counselors and they put in a heating system for us, complete with a kerosene container big enough to heat the house for the whole day (before this, the container needed to be refilled every two hours). They also filled the kerosene container in the basement. We had heat galore!

Just before dinner time, two sisters from the branch came with a hot casserole dinner and plenty of food to stock our bare shelves. We could not believe our eyes! With deep gratitude we thanked Heavenly Father for inspiring these sisters and brothers to come to our aid. Again He had shown us that He was mindful of our needs and had sent people to help us.

During an especially difficult time, Mams offered to take the children for a week to relieve us from having to buy food for the whole family. She was planning to spent a week with Annalise in Rochester and thought that it would be nice if the cousins could get acquainted. Reluctantly I agreed, and was miserable the whole time they were away. One whole week was much too long for me. Like my mother, I needed to keep my little chicks under my wings.

Just before Thanksgiving, I was able to get a job in a large department store to supplement Bob's unemployment check. Not long afterwards, Bob saw an advertisement in the newspaper that, he said, just "jumped" at him. It was for an insurance company, working in the audit and controllers department, something completely different from the work for which he had trained. Nevertheless he applied for the job and was accepted. From then on we truly "never wanted." Heavenly Father had tested our faith in Him and then had blessed us abundantly.

In time, my mother retired and spent her time visiting her children and grandchildren. When she lived with us, she attended church with us; and while visiting my brother Daniel in San Jose, California, she and his family attended each of my children's baptismal services.

During one short stay with us in San Leandro, Mams commented that she enjoyed going to church with us. She liked the Relief Society lessons during the week and enjoyed the sisterhood. She was most impressed with the sacrament service in the afternoon, and remarked upon the "special spirit" there.

Mams was pleased to see that every morning before my husband and our two older children left to teach and attend the early morning seminary classes, our family read a scripture and had a family prayer first. She was also pleased to see us ask a blessing on our food and close the day with a family prayer.

She rejoiced in the fact that we were obedient and that our religion and our callings took precedence over everything except our children.

She saw how busily we were engaged in our Heavenly Father's work. Bob served on three high councils and was a counselor in the Oakland California Mission presidency serving with two mission presidents. He had to travel and cover a large area for the Church and was often away from home, but he was always home for dinner, a happy time in our house.

When we held family nights, Mams was always invited to participate. Sometimes she read a scripture, but most of the time she preferred to furnish the treats. We had a Dutch bakery in the neighborhood and she enjoyed walking there with her granddaughter Monica to buy the treats and speak in Dutch with the congenial Dutch owners.

Mams was especially impressed that our prophet had admonished us to have a food storage on hand to use in time of need and teach us self-reliance. She was proud of the way Bob had set up our storage room, and enjoyed "shopping" in it.

Although Mams was never baptized into the Mormon church, she was moved to tears when we presented her with a Book of Mormon in Dutch. How thrilled I was when I watched her sit and read her Book of Mormon! Bob gave her a hymnbook of her own, and she faithfully brought her books to church with her—just like any other Mormon!

Many times Mams and I discussed religion, and we found that our religions had many things in common. "Have you noticed, Mams," I asked her, "that the Mormon religion is not as far 'off-the-wall' as you once thought it was? If you want to know more about it, I can have the missionaries come and teach you."

"No, thank you, my dear," she said, although she always enjoyed the company of the missionaries, who shared dinner with us at least once a week. "I believe that your God is my God, and my God is your God. Our God has stood by me in the darkest hours of my life, and I think he has approved of my life."

"Well, Mams," I teased, although I was very serious, "one year to the day after you have passed away, I will make sure that you will become a Mormon," I said, and the children chimed in, "Yes, Oma, we will do your temple work for you!"

"Well," said Mams, "you can do what you will with me after I am dead. But for now, you just leave me be!"

Chapter Thirty-Three

As the years went by, when Mams came to visit us we discovered that she was growing forgetful and was prone to do strange things. One day we could not find the frying pan, which we had used the day before. We looked everywhere for it. Then we remembered that Mams had done the dinner dishes to give the kids a "night off," so we asked her where it was. She didn't remember, even though she had washed the pan the night before.

"Don't worry," we told her, "we'll find it." And we finally did—in the linen closet in the hallway! We all laughed about this incident, but I was worried about her.

One morning, Mams decided to walk Monica to school. Mams usually came back home in fifteen minutes or so, but after an hour she still had not returned home! Concerned, I took the dog and went looking for her. When I asked the school crossing guard, Mildred, if she had seen my mother with Monica, Mildred answered, "Well, I thought it was strange that she took the other way home, but wondered if maybe she just needed something from the store." Mildred pointed towards the freeway. "She went that way," she said.

I raced home for my car and drove down the street onto the freeway. There I found Mams standing beside the busy freeway, next to a highway patrolman.

"Is this your mother?" he asked me. I nodded. "Well, she tells me she's on her way home to San Jose where she lives. Isn't that right?" he turned to my mother.

"I think so," she replied and looked at me. "Where did you come from?"

Gently I said, "You're staying with me, Mams, here in San Leandro. You took Monica to school this morning, and when you didn't come home I came looking for you."

Mams looked bewildered.

"Better take her home, lady," the patrolman said. "Take care of her."

After that, Mams would sometimes abruptly stop talking for a few seconds in the middle of a sentence, then continued on as if nothing had happened. She frequently complained of an "empty head," feeling like there was nothing in her head. I did not recognize the symptoms as the onset of Alzheimer's disease.

Mams went back to the East Coast and spent a few more years with Ellen, and alternated her visits with Konrad and Wim, who also lived in the East.

One day, Ellen called to tell me that Mam's disease had deteriorated to the point that she could no longer take care of her. It would be in everybody's best interest, she said, to have Mams admitted to a nursing home where she could get the care she needed. If everybody in the family agreed to it, Ellen would make the arrangements.

That evening Bob and I had a long talk.

"Remember," Bob reminded me, "when Mams was staying with us and was still healthy she said it was sad the way children don't take care of old people, like in the old days when families stuck together. She said, 'They put them in some nursing home, and never visit them. No wonder some nursing homes are so depressing.'"

Bob had said to her, "Listen to me, Mams. You will never end up in a nursing home. I'll take care of you myself if I have to."

And she had said, "I'll hold you to it, Bob, and I promise I'll behave myself and not give you any trouble."

So the decision was made that Mams would come to live with us.

My mother was a joy to take care of. We took her everywhere— to church, shopping, visiting, and even eating out. Of course we had to keep a constant eye on her because she had a tendency to get into mischief. She loved to walk up to people and kiss them, but people were very understanding when we explained that she had Alzheimer's.

We were fortunate that she remained sweet and kind. We heard from others that sometimes Alzheimer's patients change their personality and become very difficult to manage. The only difficulty we encountered was when we tried to clean her up after accidents or take her to the bathroom. This infringed upon her dignity, and then she would fight!

My sweet Bob was such a great help in her care. He often spoon-fed her patiently, and in the morning her cup of coffee was ready for her when we came up the stairs to the kitchen from her bedroom. Mams would gratefully sip her coffee and say, *"Lekker zeg!"* which means "Oh, this is delicious!" These words and "Thank you" were the only words she could manage to speak up to the end.

In time she lost the ability to speak, read, or write, so we had to guess what her needs were. She could not tell us when she was hungry or thirsty, cold or hot.

All of my children were of tremendous help during this time. Rick, our son, would take her on her daily walk, even after her stroke, which left her unable to walk. He'd take her in the wheelchair and "stake out the neighborhood," as he called it.

Our daughter had a special relationship with her grandmother; the two could communicate without words. Monica was always cheerful and willing to help out with her grandmother's care. When she came home from school each day, her first act was to check on her grandmother and kiss her cheek.

When Scott came home from school at BYU, he tenderly held long "conversations" with her. On his wedding day, Mams was radiant and joyously shook hands with everyone. Unfortunately, she had hidden her glasses somewhere that day and couldn't find them. But I don't think she missed them!

Our oldest daughter, Erica, was my salvation, caring for Mams when I needed a break from the constant demand of caring for an Alzheimer's patient. She, her husband, and little Valerie lived with us temporarily, which was a great blessing to me as Erica is always calm and organized. When I became flustered, she calmly took over and gave me time to regain my composure.

It was our granddaughter Valerie to whom Mams responded best. This eighteen-month-old toddler would climb on her lap with a book and "read" her great grandmother a story, or she would take a hymnbook and "sing" a song to her. She'd talk and talk to Mams, oblivious that Mams never spoke back. Or perhaps she spoke in a language only Valerie heard.

In the morning, Valerie would push open my mother's bedroom (we had taken off the lock for obvious reasons), call out "Hi, Ama!" and crawl into bed with her.

When it was time for Mam's walk with Rick, Valerie always came along, sitting on Mams' lap and holding on tightly, and off they'd go! Once in a while (really too many times to my liking!) Rick pushed the wheelchair while he ran. Valerie would squeal in delight and Mams laughed with her.

Having Mams live with us was a great honor and blessing to us. Our children learned to be considerate and compassionate, to serve and to be selfless. It brought out the best in each of them.

One day Dr. Crockett, who came to the house to care for my mother, told me that she did not have much longer. We stood quietly at the window in Mam's room as she lay dozing, in bed. "The time has come for her to leave this earth," he said.

"How long?" I asked.

"Perhaps two or three days," he said. "We can do two things. We can check her into the hospital for extended medical care, or we can keep her here at home and make her as comfortable as possible. I will leave it up to you."

"What would you do, if you were in my shoes?" I asked.

"If it were up to me," he said, "I'd keep her here at home with her loved ones nearby."

"Then we'll keep her here," I said.

We both heard Mams heave a deep sigh of relief.

"Looks like she heard your decision!" Dr. Crockett smiled at me, then turned to Mams and said gently, "You'll be all right here, Anna. We'll take good care of you."

We had two glorious days with my mother. Bob and Scott administered to her and gave her a priesthood blessing. How grateful I was to have the priesthood right here in our home! What a privilege it is to see the priesthood in action.

It was a sacred moment when Scott anointed her with oil and Bob blessed her with beautiful, comforting, loving words. Oma had not responded to anything or anyone lately, but now her eyes followed Bob as he walked to the end of the bed, and we saw that she had tears in her eyes, which then cascaded slowly down her cheeks.

Bob walked back to her side and sat down on the bed with her. He took her hand and caressed it, and she responded ever so slightly, never taking her eyes from his. His spirit had spoken to her spirit, and she had understood!

Mams passed away peacefully on July 12, 1982. I was privileged to be with her as she took her last breath and left this earth.

The next morning little Valerie opened her bedroom door and went to crawl in bed with her grandmother, but Mams was not there. Perplexed, she stood there for a moment, then looked up at me. "Where did Ama go?"

I bent my knees so that I would almost be her height and said, "Valerie, Ama has gone to Heavenly Father."

"Up there?" she pointed to the sky.

"Yes, my child, up there." She nodded her head, satisfied.

At the viewing, Valerie broke away from her mother and ran towards the casket.

"There you are!" she exclaimed. "You did not go away to heaven!"

Then turning to me and pointing to her great grandmother, she said, "See, Oma, Ama is here! She is sleeping here!" She was almost ready to crawl into the casket, then changed her mind. Erica took her by the hand, and Valerie looked up and put her fingers against her little mouth and whispered, "Shh . . . , be quiet, be very quiet, Ama is sleeping!"

We were all deeply touched by the purity and innocence of this little child, who taught us that indeed Ama was only sleeping. If we are worthy, the day will come that we will see her again. This is only a brief separation.

My brothers and sisters graciously gave me their consent to make all the arrangements for the funeral. Mams had a beautiful Mormon funeral, which greatly impressed all my brothers and sisters and my two uncles who had come to California for this occasion. We closed my mother's funeral services with her favorite scripture, which her grandchildren sang: "As I have loved you, love one another."

EPILOGUE

As I reflect on my life, I know from experience that war is never pleasant. In fact, it is a most frightening and horrifying experience. In a country where one people, or even one person, has the upper hand, it seems to be human nature that the one with the advantage must demonstrate his dominion over the other. Consequently, the oppressed may be treated unfairly and even with cruelty.

So it was during this war. However, the manner in which one accepts the circumstances or reacts to the situation makes a vast difference, perhaps not so much in *if* one will survive, but *how* one will survive. Those who have survived such an experience might well retain contempt and hatred for those who have wronged them. Such hatred cankers the soul, consumes one's life, and causes both physical and spiritual sickness.

On the other hand, when one applies the teachings of the gospel of Jesus Christ to one's life and keeps the commandments of the Lord, it is easier to "endure to the end" and survive any adversity. Those who are faithful will see the beauty and serenity of life, and find the balm of peace. They are then empowered to do good, to serve the Lord and their fellowmen, and set an example of Christlike living.

I know for a surety that Heavenly Father loves and cherishes each one of us. He knows who we are and what kind of spirits we are. He knows our characters, and is keenly aware of our strengths and weaknesses. He knows us each by name, and He can identify us from the many billions of people because He is our Heavenly Father. There is nothing that He desires more than for us to return to Him after our sojourn on this earth and live with Him again.

My parents taught me that there is a Heavenly Father who loves me and cherishes me, a Heavenly Father who sent His Only Begotten to be sacrificed, to suffer for all of our sins if we repent, even Jesus Christ who is our Savior and Redeemer. The knowledge that if I would live a righteous life, becoming a true daughter of God by taking upon me the name of Christ, I would have the influence of the Holy Ghost with me to guide, to lead, and to protect me has been the guiding force in my life.

In the Book of Mormon, the prophet Alma speaks to his son Helaman and counsels him to "never be weary of good works, but to be meek and lowly in heart. O, remember, my son, and learn wisdom in thy youth; yea, learn in thy youth to keep the commandments of God." (Alma 37:34-35.)

The scriptures teach us that unless we are humble, meek, and easy to be entreated, we are not teachable. When children are young, they are the most teachable, and those teachings will become part of their memory and will stay with them forever. "Train up a child in the way he should go: and when he is old, he will not depart from it." (Prov. 22:6.)

I have learned for myself that it is not an easy task to be a parent, but because parenthood is divinely ordained, the Lord will help us if we seek His guidance. Through my own experience, I have discovered that the parent-child relationship must be viewed as a two-way street, where parents love but children need to learn to love in return; parents counsel, but children need to want to follow the counsel; parents teach, but the children need to want to learn; parents provide, but the children need to show gratitude; parents show, but the children need to perceive; parents serve, but children need to take heed and serve as well.

When children seek, the parents will find them; when children reach out, the parents will enfold them; when children speak, parents will hear; when children knock, parents will gently guide them. At times these roles may be reversed, especially as we grow older, but it is always a give-and-take situation in an eternal partnership.

I have learned through my experience that some children prefer to exercise their agency, even at an early age. They become our challenges as they try our love and patience. They may even break our hearts with their conduct. I plead with you not to give up on them. Continue to love them with love unfeigned, with gentleness and meekness and longsuffering. (See D&C 121:41-44.) These children are merely taking a "detour" from the road to happiness and joy; it will take our constant vigil and prayers to bring them back on the path to Heavenly Father. These children have a need to test the waters for themselves, even if it means that the undertow will take them to deeper and more dangerous waters, and farther from safe shores.

We as parents need to continue to be as a beacon shining from the lighthouse to guide them back to shore, prepared to launch our lifeboat to save them, but only at their request and on their own timetable. These children choose to act this way, and this is their God-given right. We need to give them space to explore. In their behalf, let us petition our Heavenly Father daily for His mercy and His love, and then let us exercise faith, patience, and longsuffering, trusting that these wayward children will come back into the fold.

How lucky I was to have been blessed with such a mother, who taught me the ways of God in her calm, quiet, and humble manner. When I strayed, I had only to look and would always find her with a life buoy in her hand, ready to throw it to me. I could hang onto it, regain my strength, and then swim back to the safe haven of the shore, having gained another experience. How grateful I am to have had a mother who taught me correct principles, who taught me to love, to endure, to be patient. She awakened me to a sense of duty to God. Clothed and armed with this knowledge that the gospel of Jesus Christ is a pattern for our lives, I was prepared to face life and its challenges.

I cherish the fact that I am a woman, created spiritually by my Heavenly Father, and physically by an earthly father and mother. I am grateful to have been placed on this earth to fulfill the measure of my creation, to be a true and faithful daughter in Zion, and to "multiply and replenish the earth . . . and to fulfill the promise which was given [to all women] by [our] Father before the foundation of the world . . . that [we] may bear the souls of men: for herein is the work of [our] Father continued, that he may be glorified." (D&C 132:63.)

This scripture has comforted me so much over the years, because it shows me how just our Heavenly Father is. This promise is for all women, whether we are now married or not. Since the Lord is perfect, He has created a perfect plan of salvation in which there will be a place in the gospel for the married, widowed, single, or childless woman. Perhaps not all will be given in this life, but certainly in the life hereafter. I know this, because He has promised it. "For behold, this is my work and my glory—to bring to pass the immortality and eternal life of man." (Moses 1:39.)

While on this earth, it behooves us to acquire the skills to become good mothers by developing our inborn talents of nurturing, to expand our compassionate service, to deepen our understanding of the scriptures, to prove ourselves faithful and true, and to bring honor to the sanctity of womanhood.

I know that the fullness of the gospel of Jesus Christ has been restored in these latter days, and in this we have been given the freedom and the power to act, and to speak and to think without restraint of the goodness and mercy of God. He has given us the gift of agency, a most precious gift, and with this gift He expects us to govern our own lives, to choose good or evil, to be obedient or disobedient. He waits patiently, hoping and exercising great faith in us that we will each choose good over evil.

Of course, we must do our part. Our contribution is required through the process of repentance, by forsaking all sins to be able to partake of this freedom fully and to experience joy and gain eternal life. Through Christ's atoning sacrifice we have been freed from the oppression of the Adversary, who in stark contrast and opposition came up with the plan to force us to do the things required to come back to our Heavenly Father and Jesus Christ, thereby taking away our freedom. May I plead with you to appreciate your freedom that we may be a caring people, that we may overcome our prejudices, that we may develop tolerance so we may become a charitable people, rich and strong in that charity that is so eloquently described by the ancient prophet Moroni: "And charity suffereth long, and is kind, and envieth not, and is not puffed up, seeketh not her own, is not easily provoked, thinketh no evil, and rejoiceth not in iniquity but rejoiceth in the truth, beareth all things, believeth all things, hopeth all things, endureth all things." (Moro. 7:45.)

The Lord has said, "My people must be tried in all things that they may be prepared to receive the glory that I have for them." (D&C 136:31.) In John 16:30 Jesus said, "In this world ye shall have tribulations."

Trials and tribulations come to all of us. We do not ask for them. But "after much tribulation come the blessings. Wherefore the day cometh that ye shall be crowned with much glory; the hour is not yet, but is nigh at hand." (D&C 58:4.)

The Lord has promised us: "Draw near unto me and I will draw near unto you; seek me diligently and ye shall find me; ask, and ye shall receive; knock, and it shall be opened unto you." (D&C 88:63.) During our most trying and difficult times, my family drew near unto the Lord and we felt that He was near us. We sought Him diligently and we found Him, we asked and we received, we knocked and He opened a door for us.

In time of trouble let us then remember the comforting words from the Lord Jesus Christ when he said: "Peace I leave with you, my peace I give unto you: not as the world giveth, give I unto you. Let not your heart be troubled, neither let it be afraid." (John 14:20.) "Learn of me . . . and ye shall find rest unto your souls." (Matt. 11:29.)

That we may all learn to do so, and receive the Lord's comfort and loving guidance, is my earnest hope and prayer.

ABOUT THE AUTHOR

Kitty de Ruyter was born in Semarang, on the island of Java, in Indonesia, where she lived until immigrating with her family to Holland. There Kitty graduated from high school and attended a teachers' college, although a second immigration, this time to the United States, interrupted her studies at the teachers' college. In the U.S., she continued her studies in Connecticut and later in California.

Her beloved Bob was unable to accompany her for almost two years, and he remained in Holland where he met the LDS missionaries and was baptized into The Church of Jesus Christ of Latter-day Saints. When he joined Kitty in the U.S., she attended church with Bob and investigated the Church for two years before finally accepting baptism at the age of 26.

Kitty and Bob raised their family mostly in California, where Bob served as a counselor in the mission presidency and as a high councilman. Kitty herself also served in a variety of callings for the Church including stake and ward Young Women's president, Primary president and teacher, and Gospel Doctrine teacher. She has the distinction of having survived fifteen girls' camps. She has taught Relief Society and is currently her ward Relief Society president.

In 1989 Kitty was awarded the Distinguished Freedom Award by the city of Provo, Utah, for "love of country and contribution in unselfishly giving of [her] time and talent." Similar awards were given at the same time to President Ezra Taft Benson and BYU president Rex E. Lee. She was also recognized by Lambda Delta Sigma with the "Elect Lady" award.

Kitty has been invited to speak to a broad range of audiences—from U.S. servicemen and women to students at Ricks College and Utah State College. She has also spoken at the Church Education Symposium, Especially for Youth, the LDS Singles Conference, and the LDS Hearing Impaired Conference. She has been a lecturer at both the Salt Lake Community College and at the University of Utah Institute of Religion.

Kitty and her husband, Bob, have four children and ten grandchildren. She enjoys spending time with her family and grandchildren, doing handwork such as knitting and embroidering, cooking Indonesian food, and reading and studying the scriptures.